Contents

Acknowledgements

We are very grateful to all those who helped with this report. They include all the individuals in the organisations which kindly took part in this research. We would also like to thank: members of the advisory group; Barbara Ballard at the Joseph Rowntree Foundation; and Shirley Dex, the Programme Adviser, for their contributions and encouragement. Also, our thanks to colleagues at the ERI and, in particular, Matt Smith for his contributions to the project.

1 | Introduction

The context for family-friendly policies

Paid work can be family unfriendly. Typically, it has taken place away from domestic surroundings and, for many, may require long and increasingly uncertain travel times. Further, paid work has been subject to the dictates of the clock, provided on a 'take it or leave it' 9.00 to 5.00 basis for office staff, clashing with school or nursery times, or often on an 'unsocial' shift basis for men. Overtime would be available (and indeed desirable to offset low manual worker pay) but unpredictable in its provision. Even today, it is recognised that the UK has a long-hours working culture: between 1988 and 1998, the proportion of men working more than 50 hours a week rose from 24 to 30 per cent and the proportion of women from 4 to 10 per cent (Harkness, 1999, p. 93). Growing insecurity among professional, technical and managerial occupations has exacerbated the tendency for people to demonstrate their organisational 'commitment' by their continual presence at the workplace (*Management Today*, 2000; Simpson, 2000). For many women with families, choices have been even more restricted and dominated by economic inactivity or low-paid part-time working.

Nevertheless, recent years have witnessed a number of significant, albeit incremental, shifts within UK society that impact upon the boundaries between work and family. First, there have been growing pressures for greater gender equality both in and out of work. These pressures have been expressed in legislation designed to remove pay inequalities and discriminatory barriers between men and women; escalation in the numbers of women with high level educational qualifications and professional status; and under these circumstances growing attention to the unequal burdens undertaken by men and women over domestic responsibilities.

Second, the structures of family life have been evolving, with the gradual decline of the extended family and increasing numbers of lone-parent households (Crow and Hardey, 1999). Contemporaneously, demands for elder care have grown with both longer life expectancy and greater emphasis upon community rather than institutional care. Third, the economy has been shifting to sectors with emphasis on service provision, both in public and private sectors. One consequence of this shift has been the expansion of the proportions of women in work, especially in the service sector. Fourth, there have been significant changes in the political make-up of the UK. With the change in government in 1997 emerged an expanded number of women MPs in Parliament. Possibly as a consequence, family issues have risen higher on the policy agenda with the establishment of a number of family-focused government think tanks and policy bodies accompanied by political pursuit of family-orientated agendas.

Alongside the growth of political pressures, supportive legislation, awareness of opportunities or the lack of them and, subsequently, swelling numbers of well educated women moving into paid employment has grown a debate on ways to match economic needs with domestic needs, and especially with the needs of children. On the one hand, it is held to be economically, socially and personally desirable for men and women to have equal access to work. Indeed, there are now substantial political and financial pressures for all potentially economically active people to gain paid employment. On the other hand, there are concerns of the deleterious effects on children and their development of parental (and specifically maternal) absence during the early years of childhood (see, for example, Ermisch and Francesconi, 2001). Researchers, if not policy-makers, are becoming increasingly aware of the potential negative consequences of domestic lives disrupted by unpredictable shift patterns, irregular overtime demands and work intrusions into the quality of home life through heightened levels of stress, insecurity and exhaustion (Baldry et al., 2000; Hyman et al., 2001).

Recently, tightening labour market conditions have increased employer concerns that, in order to attract and retain staff, they must be prepared to offer working conditions that might appeal to the broadest possible eligible labour population, including people with family commitments. An added inducement to companies to offer family-friendly employment is provided by the 'business case' in that qualitative or behavioural improvements in employee performance have been reported in organisations where such arrangements have been introduced (see, for example, Dex and Scheibl, 1999).

Against this background, the past five years have witnessed an intensifying debate over contemporary contours of the family friendliness of work for the following reasons:

- Organisations face greater pressures to respond to service market signals in an environment of intense domestic and international competitiveness. Responses include more flexible opening times, attention to service quality and the need to recruit and retain scarce skills in order to provide appropriate levels of service.

- Under these turbulent market conditions, organisations need both committed and readily available workforces to extend the parameters of both the working day and the working week. Many employers have introduced regimes of time flexibility in the belief that this will engage positively with employee need and consequently with their commitment.

- The Government has introduced legislation of an enabling kind, encouraging *voluntary* initiatives (supported by base-line statutory unpaid provision) on paternity, parental, and domestic emergency leave arrangements to be determined between employers and their employees and/or their representatives.

- Increasing concerns about the pressures of contemporary work patterns and practices on working parents and their relationships with their families; growing numbers of men are apparently seeking to reduce working hours in order to spend more time with their families (see, for example, Lewis and Lewis, 1996).

The growth in interest in family-friendly employment

As we noted above, accelerating changes at work and in society over the past decade have led to increased policy and research attention to the interactions between employment and domestic life. The main dimensions to current policy and research interest have been directed towards examination of the ways used by employers to help balance working and domestic lives of employees; and the effects of providing greater flexibility and balanced work arrangements on employees' domestic lives and on work performance.

With regard to the first area, the 1998 Workplace Employee Relations Survey (WERS) indicated that 60 per cent of all workplaces had in place one or more of the following practices:

- home working during normal working hours

- term-time working

- switch from full-time to part-time employment

- job sharing.

The most common practice was 'the ability to switch from full-time to part-time employment' (Cully *et al.*,1999, p. 75), reported by just over half the workplaces. All entitlements were more common in the public sector, with half of all private sector companies offering none of these entitlements. The WERS study also demonstrates that, prior to the Employment Relations Act 1999 (see section on 'Government support for family-friendly employment policies' below), most employers reported that they would allow staff time off for domestic emergencies. Leave was likely to be paid in the public sector but in the private sector: 'the onus is largely on the employee to bear the cost of the absence' in one way or another (Cully *et al.*, 1999, p. 76). The present research explores the extent to which this position has altered in the finance services sector following the introduction of the 1999 Act.

The Work–Life Balance Baseline Study (Hogarth *et al.*, 2000) also produced some interesting findings regarding employers' attitudes and practices. Many employers expressed sympathy to notions of 'work–life balance' without actually saying what these were, or doing very much to secure balance. For example, most workplaces had employees working in excess of standard working hours, often unpaid. Those 'most likely to work long hours were men in couple households with

dependent children'. Fourteen per cent of these worked at least 60 hours a week (Hogarth *et al.*, 2000). The employer survey for the study indicated a 'not high' incidence of flexible working time arrangements, other than flexibility over working hours and part-time employment.

The WERS study also asked employees about their perceptions of employer family-friendly provisions, enquiring about their 'personal access' to five different kinds of flexible and family-friendly provisions (Cully *et al.*, 1999, p. 144). These include:

- flexible working hours

- job share

- home working during normal working hours

- parental leave

- workplace nursery or child-care assistance.

Slightly more than half the employees cited the availability of at least one of these provisions. The most commonly available arrangement was flexible working hours (32 per cent) especially among clerical and secretarial employees. Job sharing (16 per cent) and home working (9 per cent) were less commonly available. In common with other studies, employer assistance with child care was mentioned by only a tiny minority of respondents. Just over one-quarter of respondents reported access to parental leave. All the above provisions were reported more frequently in the public sector. Also, women were more likely than men to report access to each of the provisions. Also positively associated with reported access were: level of education; and perceptions of job influence. Reported access to time off for emergency dependent care was common, with employees

Research Problem

often subsequently making up time. About half of the respondents claimed that time off was paid, though the study did not make clear whether this was through special paid leave or by using holiday (or other) entitlements. The present study examines this issue of time off for dependant care in greater depth.

Further, the employee survey for the Baseline Study also demonstrated little evidence of 'significant take up of flexible working time arrangements … other than flexitime and part-time working' despite 'considerable latent demand for flexible working arrangements' (Hogarth et al., 2000, p. 11). Employers were not especially well informed about family-friendly developments: only one in five had detailed knowledge of new maternity leave regulations and one in four of parental leave regulations. Only a small minority of these provided benefits above the statutory minimum.

Hogarth et al. also provided details on the extent and effects of workplace consultation. Consultation over working hours was found to be common, especially in large unionised concerns, and where consultation over working arrangements was found: 'the incidence of flexible working practices increases'. Unfortunately, the study treated 'management decision' and 'after consultation' as mutually exclusive categories (Hogarth et al. 2000, p. 30), even though the usual definition of consultation assumes that management makes the decision unilaterally, though possibly informed with contributions from employee representatives. The extent to which employees and their representatives can or do influence management decisions is explored in depth in the current study.

Finally, the Baseline Study signals positive outcomes for organisations, with three-quarters of workplace managers agreeing with statements that work–life balance fostered good employment relations and nearly half agreeing that staff are happier. The extent to which these same respondents actually exercise work–life balance arrangements, or the ways in which they practise these were not stated. Nevertheless, there appears to be a *belief* among employers of net positive effects of establishing balanced work arrangements.

Other studies have examined potential benefits to employers in more detail (Dex and Scheibl, 1999). Retention and recruitment, direct productivity effects and enhanced employee commitment and morale have been identified as positive outcomes of support for staff and especially for working parents. In one major survey, over three-quarters of employers pointed to at least one benefit associated with flexible working and leave arrangements (DTI, 2000). Nevertheless, anticipated (though rarely quantified) cost appears to be the single biggest constraint on employer commitment to further advances (DTI, 2000, p. 77).

Despite apparent limited progress towards support for working parents and for employees generally, differences between what employees want and what business organisations feel they can afford are apparent. According to research, only 3 per cent of parents have taken unpaid parental leave under the regulations introduced in December 1999 (*Bargaining Report*, 2001, p. 13). Leave without pay, especially with the added expense of child care, is not an option, it seems, for many workers. In a study of 152 union representatives, the most welcome entitlement (70 per cent) would be the introduction of paid parental leave. Also desirable would be an increase in the length of statutory maternity pay to 26 weeks (57 per cent); rights for both parents to reduce hours after maternity leave; paid paternity leave;

entitlement to time off for hospital appointments involving dependants (all 51 per cent) (*Labour Research*, 2001).

It seems that the Government is addressing at least some of these issues. In the 2001 Budget statement, the Chancellor announced that the standard rate of maternity pay is to rise from £60 to £75 (2002) and then to £100 by year 2003. Paid maternity leave is to be extended from 18 weeks to 26 weeks and, from April 2003, two weeks' paid paternity leave (also at £100 a week) is to be introduced.

Government support for family-friendly employment policies

The Employment Relations Act 1999 provided important new collective and individual rights for employees. Recognising the pressures facing the 4.5 million employed women and 5.5 million employed men with family commitments (Labour Research Department, 2000, p. 3), as well as those with family responsibilities wishing to enter employment, the Government published the Maternity and Parental Leave Regulations to take effect from December 1999. Whilst the improved maternity rights build upon existing legislation, rights to parental leave and time off for dependants derive from EU directives and represent new legal rights in the UK (Labour Research Department, 2000). Two approaches are available for parental leave. The first is the so-called fallback scheme, which outlines the minimum levels available to employees who have completed at least one year of service with an employer. Alternatively, the Regulations positively encourage collective or individual agreements on parental leave to be established providing that these at least meet the minimum rights to leave offered by the fallback scheme. There is no requirement for employees to take

leave and, under the Regulations, leave is unpaid, unless provision is made for any payment through the agreement. There is, therefore, substantial encouragement for employers and employees to establish their own parental leave arrangements, backed by the minimum requirements of the fallback scheme. As the Labour Research Department Guide points out:

> As such, trade unions and workplace negotiators in particular, have a key role to play in improving the basic entitlements contained in the regulations.
> (Labour Research Department, 2000, p. 5)

The same Regulations also provide all employees with the protected right to take off 'a reasonable period of time' to deal with dependant emergency situations. The sorts of occasions where this right might apply have been summarised by the Department of Trade and Industry (DTI) and include paternity leave, child-care emergencies and sickness. There is no statutory right to pay but the DTI advises that 'whether the employee will be paid is left to the employer's discretion, or to the contract of employment between them' (Labour Research Department, 2000).

The Government has also given exhortatory support through the Department for Education and Employment (DfEE) Work–Life Balance Campaign and elsewhere to encourage greater flexibility in employment conditions. Encouragement is being offered for easier access to movement between full- and part-time work, term-time working and other non-statutory initiatives for staff with dependent family commitments. Further, as we noted from the Budget details above, the Government intends to add new entitlements for working parents.

The scope for discretion

At the time of the research in 2000, the Government's family-friendly employment policies consisted of a statutory entitlement to unpaid parental leave and a statutory right to take unpaid time off to deal with a family emergency. The policy also provided employers with the scope to offer alternative models, providing that minimum statutory levels of entitlement are offered. These conditions apply to the initiatives shown in Table 1, which outlines the ways in which minimum statutory provisions may be exceeded or where additional related benefits that extend beyond the statutory framework may be offered:

In addition to the initiatives shown in Table 1, there are a number of other ways in which employment may be structured to assist employees with domestic commitments. These are usually related to employment flexibility and the principal components are as follows:

- part-time working

- full-time–part-time interchangeability

- flexible working hours

- flexitime

- job share

Table 1   Statutorily backed and other family-friendly initiatives (at end 2000)

Initiative	Scope for discretion
Maternity provisions	Scope for companies to offer enhanced maternity leave and/or pay beyond statutory requirements.
Parental leave	Statutory minimum entitlement is for 13 weeks' unpaid leave for each child up to age of five years for children born after 15 December 1999. Scope to offer paid leave and improvement of minimum entitlement conditions.
Paternity leave	Implied statutory right to unpaid leave for fathers only usually at time of child's birth. Scope to offer paid leave and to raise amount of time granted to fathers.
Time off for dependants (TOFD)	ERA 1999 offers statutory right to all employees to take a reasonable time off work to deal with an emergency involving a dependant. No statutory right to pay and no time limit set by ERA.
Compassionate leave	No statutory right offered (unless it is the death of a dependant, which is covered by the TOFD regulations above). Usually time off to deal with death or serious illness of close friend or relative. Scope to offer pay, limit number of days and broaden range of dependent situations.
Other leave	No statutory backing, e.g. marriage leave.

- term-time contracts

- home working.   *This Study*

The intention in the study is to explore the policies adopted by companies in the finance sector. In particular, this approach will offer insights into the extent to which companies have shifted beyond the statutory minimum for family-friendly arrangements and the factors that have prompted them to take these voluntary actions.

Organisational decision-making and employee participation

Strategic organisational decisions are usually the responsibility of senior management. At policy and operational levels, however, there are persuasive arguments that employees 'should have a say in decisions which directly affect them' (CBI, 1990). Employee participation in organisational decision-making can be justified in a number of ways:

- It represents a democratic right of employees (Bean, 1994).

- Participative decision-making leads to better decisions (DTI, 1997).

- Areas of disagreement or misunderstandings between the parties can be identified and resolved.

- Many employers, as well as successive governments, have also been persuaded that forms of employee participation in organisational decision-making are an appropriate approach to capture employee commitment and loyalty (DTI, 1997).

There are two generic approaches to participation, each with a number of variants. First, there is *direct* participation between individual employees and individual managers.

For its advocates, direct participation has the merit that an intervening body does not act between the employee and his or her manager. Examples would include performance appraisal, suggestion schemes and staff attitude surveys (see Cully *et al.*, 1999).

Indirect participation allows for the introduction of a representative body to act collectively on behalf of individual employees. Approaches include:

- joint consultation

- works councils

- collective bargaining over terms and conditions of employment.

Independent trade unions are more likely to extend participative activities to collective bargaining than in-house staff associations. The role of the latter tends to be restricted to more informational and consultative activities, potentially because of their dependence upon the host organisation. Collective bargaining is a preferred participative approach of trade unions as it assumes 'some sharing of power' (Cully *et al.*, 1999, p. 64) with management, whilst consultation tends to be more inclined to unilateral management decision-making but with some input by the representative body into the decision.

Indirect approaches may overcome the chief potential objection to direct participation in that, without representation, individual employees may lack the informational or bargaining resources to participate on an equal footing with their superiors in the organisation. For this reason, supporters argue that indirect or representative participation not only diminishes employment relationship inequalities, but can lead to better informed decisions to which all parties will willingly abide. Leading on from this are claims that indirect participation can boost organisational performance.

It is also suggested by many that where independent trade unions are recognised by the company a further layer of legitimacy is added to the authority of joint decision-making processes. Indeed, it could be argued that the time is appropriate for unions to both raise the banner of family-friendly work policies and to influence their coverage, depth and operation at the workplace. Trade unions also need to confront family-friendly employment issues: they not only wish to demonstrate their appreciation of domestic pressures to members and potential members but also need to show that they can do something positive about them at a time when they are faced with little scope for pay bargaining because of continuing low inflation rates. More fundamentally, unions are seeking ways to enhance their attraction and relevance to members as they emerge from their 20-year enforced decline. Understandably, then, a number of trade unions have also expressed their commitment to addressing issues of work–life balance through negotiation with employers or through other representative means.

There is little doubt that unions have previously grasped opportunities to couple welfare reform to their workplace role. Unions were instrumental in the introduction of occupational pensions reform and have participated enthusiastically (if not always too effectively) in many company and industry pensions trusts. Health and safety protection of employees has traditionally been a role that unions have embraced, especially when supported by legislation. In more recent years, unions have extended this protectionist role

into opposition to workplace bullying and harassment. There is, in short, good reason to examine the impact that unions are exerting on family-friendly policies as this is an area where, supported directly by governmental polices and indirectly by positive social concerns, they might legitimately be able to influence policy and practice. With regard to the former, there is early evidence that positive general effects in terms of entitlement can be associated with trade union presence (see *Bargaining Report*, 2000; *Equal Opportunities Review*, 2000; Hogarth *et al.*, 2000, p. 31). But entitlement of course does not mean that people can or do act on their entitlements. One of the intentions of the case study phase of the present research has been to examine the extent to which practice, stimulated by trade unions or not, follows the policies that have been established.

The aims of the project

Notwithstanding these current high levels of interest in family-friendly or family-responsive employment policies (FFPs), there is a shortage of evidence available over the sort of arrangements introduced; the types of organisations in which they have been introduced; and, in particular, the roles of employees and managers in helping to introduce, maintain and improve arrangements. An examination of these issues and their relationships forms the principal aim of the present study. The research team was especially concerned to examine the processes and depths to which employees and their representative bodies were able to influence family-friendly employment through both direct and indirect forms of participation.

Clearly, there are numerous potential strands to work–family links. These strands multiply if concerns are extended to work–life balance generally. With policy and debate focused largely on parenting issues, for this study we have decided to concentrate primarily on these aspects rather than on extending the research to the equally important issues of elder care or the care of disabled dependants.

The general aims of the study can be disaggregated to a number of sub-aims:

- To examine existing arrangements for the provision of voluntary family-friendly benefits by employers in a key sector (financial services) in Scotland.

- To identify, from this data, the influence of employee participation on family-friendly provision.

- To identify whether there are differences between formal provision of benefits and informal practices, and, if so, to explore the reasons for this.

- To inform organisational practice about varieties and impacts of different approaches to family-friendly provision and practice.

- To inform policy-makers and practitioners about impacts of current voluntary provisions.

- To examine whether different patterns of provision have differential impacts upon groups of employees and the extent to which there is equality of access.

Methodology

The financial services sector

The research team selected the *financial services sector* for the study. The principal justification for choosing this sector was that, among employers, the finance sector has gained a reputation for progressive employment policies. The finance sector was at the forefront in introducing child-care or 'family-responsive' arrangements for staff, or for prospective staff, during the 1990s. In addition:

- The sector is a major and vibrant industry employing large numbers of women (Cully *et al.*, 1999, p. 25).

- The companies are keen to reflect a family-friendly image to customers or potential customers.

- There are different representative arrangements for employee participation ranging from no formal representative arrangements; through in-house staff associations; to formally agreed joint regulatory arrangements with independent TUC-affiliated trade unions.

- It is a highly competitive and turbulent sector facing issues of merger, demutualisation and rapidly changing markets.

- The labour market for staff is very tight and employers may adopt family-focused employment policies to compete for scarce staff.

If we are to seek evidence for developments in the introduction of diverse or advanced forms of family-friendly policies, we might reasonably expect to find them in this sector. From this evidence, it may be possible to identify initiatives, processes and outcomes which might serve as guides to employers in other sectors as well as to policy-makers and other stakeholders with an interest in this area.

The research was deliberately confined to Scotland, though many of the organisations studied have large operations in the rest of the UK and beyond. Nevertheless, many of the finance sector's head offices are based in Scotland, giving the research team access to corporate (or at the very least regional) headquarters. The financial services sector (comprising banking and finance, insurance and auxiliary activities) in Scotland directly employed 73,500 people in 1997 in 815 enterprises. Of the 73,500 people employed, about three-quarters were female (*Scottish Abstract of Statistics*, 1998) and about one-fifth of the women were designated as part-time.

Phase 1: company and trade union surveys

Forty finance sector companies with an administrative base in Scotland were approached through telephone and letter to take part in an initial survey of their family-friendly policies and arrangements. Seventeen companies agreed to participate within the narrow timescale available for this phase of the research. Commencing in January 2000 and concluding in September, studies of the FFP arrangements in these 17 finance sector organisations were undertaken as the first phase of the study. Each organisational study included in-depth face-to-face interviews with relevant managerial staff. A questionnaire checklist was also carried out mapping the components of the family-friendly provisions. Formal documentation such as agreements, staff handbooks, annual reports, etc. was also requested. In a separate but related exercise, interviews with senior officials of seven trade unions with recognition rights in the finance sector were also conducted.

For the first phase, the following data from 17 companies were gathered through the methods described above:

- impetus for the introduction of FFPs, with particular emphasis on the roles of employees and their representative institutions

- processes of introduction (e.g. consultation, negotiation, joint working parties, management alone) and maintenance (e.g. monitoring)

 coverage of FFPs in terms of both contents and potential and actual beneficiaries

- nature of provisions available to employees

- contributions of trade unions and union representatives

- signs of pressures from different sources to develop/expand/modify/curtail the FF programme.

Together with the findings from union officials, we assess the value of voluntary initiatives in this area of employee welfare. Both phases of the study pay particular reference to the role of trade unions, many of which have entered into currently fashionable 'partnership' arrangements with employers in the finance sector. As we saw above, unions have traditionally promoted their welfare responsibilities and it will be of value to review the extent to which this orientation is inserted into current employment relations policies and practices. Any differences in perspective between trade unions and employers over meanings and scope of FFPs are also discussed.

Phase 2: company case studies

The second phase was conducted between June 2000 and January 2001. This phase consisted of more intensive examination of four diverse case study organisations drawn from the first phase. The case studies involved an examination of how FFPs operate in practice, looking closely at micro-level decision-making and employee responses. Full details of the company case study methodology are presented in Chapter 4.

Structure of the report

Following this introductory chapter, the report is presented in two parts.

- Part I, covering Chapters 2 and 3, deals with policy formation and presents evidence from Phase 1 of the project, mainly relating to macro-level decisions to introduce FFPs in the 17 companies. Chapters 2 and 3 cover findings from the company and union surveys respectively.

- Part II, covering Chapters 4 to 9, examines the ways in which policy is translated into practice. This draws on data drawn primarily from the four case studies.

Chapter 4 introduces the four case study companies and contains details of the methodology for the four detailed case studies.

Chapter 5 looks at the process of policy development and introduction and the level of formal provision in each of the four companies. We then look at how these policies were communicated to line managers. The effectiveness of communication and management training is tested by examining managerial awareness over FFPs.

Chapter 6 explores the ways in which managers make decisions in the operation of family-friendly policies and the constraints they experience. The research examines:

- tensions between formal policies and the exercise of managerial discretion

- organisational factors that may act as barriers or facilitators to the operation of policies

- other criteria employed that may affect the outcome of the decision-making process.

Next, bearing in mind that the current aim of government policy is to encourage voluntarily agreed arrangements that meet or exceed statutory levels of FFP provision, Chapter 7 examines the extent to which managerial decision-making is subject to direct and indirect participative influences.

Chapter 8 examines employee experiences of family-friendly policies and the ways policies and practices outlined in the previous chapters affect employees. In particular the report examines:

- employee awareness of FFPs and their source of information

- the take-up of FFPs and how managerial decision-making affects usage

- employee access to different forms of leave and flexible working practices.

Chapter 9 investigates the companies' overall family-friendly orientations through:

- perceived relations between employees and managers

- influence on employee retention by the provision of FFPs

- employee understandings of and attitudes towards company FFPs.

Chapter 10 brings together the conclusions to the study and their implications for companies, trade unions and policy-makers.

Part I

Policy formation

2 | Company survey findings

The Phase I companies

The 17 organisations interviewed in the first phase of the study together employed over 50,000 staff in Scotland. Only two of the companies had their headquarters located outside Scotland. With the exception of these two companies, all the companies had their head offices located in the central belt of Scotland. The two non-Scottish companies also had their regional headquarters located in the central belt. Head offices were located mostly in Edinburgh with a smaller number in Glasgow. All interviews for companies based in Scotland were conducted at the head offices where the frameworks for the policies were established. The mean number of employees per organisation in Scotland was 2,970. The smallest establishment employed just over 100 people in Scotland and the largest over 10,000. From the companies that provided data, the mean proportion of women employed in the companies was 58 per cent and the average age of employees was 33.6 years. Four banks are included, seven insurance/assurance (Insur/ Assur), one general finance (Fin) with strong mortgage interests and five fund managers (FM). Employment patterns in the 17 companies are shown in Table 2.

Table 3 shows the profiles of union and staff association recognition for companies in this sample. The patterns of employee representation reflect the traditions of the finance sector in respect of both the assurance companies and the banks. Banking institutions

Table 2 Number of employees in the survey companies

	Scotland	Rest of UK	Worldwide	Total
Assur 1	506	0	0	506
Assur 2	9,000	0	0	9,000
Assur 3	2,100	0	0	2,100
Assur 4	990	286	0	1,276
Assur 5	*	1,600	0	1,600
Assur 6	3,100	400	0	3,500
Insur 1	2,800	7,400	800	11,000
Bank 1	12,000	8,000	2,000	22,000
Bank 2	6,000	*	50,000	56,000
Bank 3	4,000	68,264	4,000	76,264
Bank 4	10,000	99,000	Not indicated	109,000
FM 1	298	4	1	303
FM 2	210	8	4	222
FM 3	204	6	3	213
FM 4	150	50	100	300
FM 5	110	0	0	110
Fin 1	*	36,000	0	36,000

Source: Company statistics.

*Disaggregated figures not available.

Table 3 Trade union recognition and staff association presence in the sample companies

	Union	Staff association
Assur 1	MSF	
Assur 2		Yes
Assur 3		Yes
Assur 4		Yes
Assur 5		Yes
Assur 6	MSF	
Insur 1		Yes
Bank 1	Unifi	
Bank 2	Unifi	
Bank 3	Unifi	Yes
Bank 4	Unifi	
FM 1		
FM 2		
FM 3		
FM 4		
FM 5		
Fin 1	Company-based union*	

*TUC recognised.

have tended to recognise trade unions, with Unifi (ex-BIFU) being the dominant union. Staff associations, unaffiliated to the TUC, have dominated the insurance/assurance sector, though some companies recognise the Manufacturing, Science and Finance Union (MSF). In other cases, recent shifts from in-house staff association to TUC-recognised trade union have taken place. There was neither trade union recognition nor staff association presence in any of the five fund managers included in the study. Again, this characteristic is not unusual in small, independent, private sector service organisations.

FFP provision and union presence

During the first phase of the study, we asked company respondents whether they had introduced any of the family-friendly polices (FFPs) or flexible working practices (FWPs) indicated in Tables 4 and 5. In order to illustrate the patterns of provisions, we have classified the companies according to their form of employee representation available, i.e. union recognised (7), staff association (5), or no formal employee representation (5).

Table 4 illustrates three main points. First, where unions are recognised, there were more likely to be voluntary initiatives across the FFP spectrum. These initiatives included two companies that, with their unions, had jointly agreed the removal of the December 1999 cut-off date for parental leave. Second, FFP initiatives were less commonly found in those companies with in-house staff associations. Third, smaller independent finance houses without any formal systems of employee representation offered some enhancements beyond the statutory requirements.

Companies were also asked about their arrangements for other kinds of family-friendly leave, dividing these into time off for dependants (TOFD) and compassionate leave. TOFD is a statutory right under ERA 1999, which gives all employees the right to take a reasonable period of time off work to deal with an emergency related to a dependent relative. There is no right to pay and no formal time limit. Table 5 details the arrangements offered by these 17 companies.

The provision of TOFD is difficult to analyse because of the potential variety of circumstances that might be included. Nevertheless, a pattern of sorts does emerge. More generous provisions were offered subject

Table 4 FFPs and presence of employee representation

	Enhanced parental leave	Enhanced maternity leave	Enhanced maternity pay	Maternity returner bonus	Paid paternity leave
Union recognised					
Bank 1	✓	✓			
Bank 2			✓		✓
Bank 3	✓	✓			✓
Bank 4		✓			✓
Fin 1	✓		✓		✓
Assur 1	✓			✓	✓
Assur 6				✓	✓
Staff associations					
Insur 1					✓
Assur 2			✓		✓
Assur 3			✓		✓
Assur 4					✓
Assur 5				✓	✓
No representation					
FM 1	Under review	✓	✓		✓
FM 2		✓	✓		✓
FM 3			✓		✓
FM 4				✓	
FM 5			✓		✓

to management discretion in finance houses without employee representation. Rather more formal and codified systems, though perhaps more restrictive, operated in those companies recognising trade unions, whilst the staff association companies tended to follow little more than the statutory requirement of allowing time off without pay.

Compassionate leave, usually involving time off for the death or serious illness of a relative or close friend, is one category that is not formally covered by statute. Details of provision are offered in Table 6. No distinctive patterns of provision emerge: most of the companies did offer some paid leave, with the length of the paid absence left to the discretion of individual managers. Even so, some of the companies harboured considerable concerns about codifying areas such as compassionate leave:

The danger is that people saw that five-day compassionate as an entitlement and added it onto their annual holiday leave. You know, 'I haven't had my five days' compassionate leave.'

(Senior manager for employment policy, Bank 2)

Table 5 Time off for dependants (TOFD)

Arrangement offered by company

Union recognised

Bank 1	Unpaid. Encourage use of flexitime and holidays.
Bank 2	Up to five days paid. Formal entitlement but operation discretionary.
Bank 3	Maximum three days paid.
Bank 4	Paid on discretionary basis. No details.
Fin 1	Paid at manager's discretion. No details.
Assur 1	First day paid of each leave period. Rest unpaid.
Assur 6	Statutory minimum, but staff directed to take holidays.

Staff associations

Insur 1	Unpaid.
Assur 2	Unpaid (formal); (informal) paid leave at management discretion.
Assur 3	Sickness – use holidays if want paid. If used, discretion of manager. Care breakdown – use holidays or up to five days paid.
Assur 4	Unclear if paid or not.
Assur 5	Unpaid.

No representation

FM 1	Paid at management discretion.
FM 2	First two days paid for each leave period. Rest unpaid.
FM 3	Paid at management discretion.
FM 4	Paid at management discretion.
FM 5	No formal policy.

A number of miscellaneous provisions were on offer by different companies. Three offered paid military leave;[1] one offered five days' paid marriage leave provided the marriage was recognised by the State; one offered paid time off for fertility treatment and another for moving house. One company offered paid study days for staff taking professional exams.

With regard to direct support for child care, only four companies, all with recognised trade unions, had taken tentative steps in this direction. One bank had introduced a pilot nursery place scheme, where the bank paid so many hours per month at the nursery.

However, they were thinking of abandoning the scheme because of 'absolutely terrible take-up'. Another bank offered child-care vouchers as an option in its flexible benefits scheme. An assurance company included interest-free salary advances for child-care costs. A fourth company was reviewing potential child-care support options.

A similar exercise for identifying provision was undertaken for the presence of the various types of arrangement under the heading of flexible working practices (FWPs). For these, with the exception of term-time contracts, a rather more extensive pattern emerged as shown in Table 7.

Table 6 Compassionate leave provision

	Provision
Union recognised	
Bank 1	Formal policy – up to five days paid at manager's discretion.
Bank 2	Formal policy – up to five days paid.
Bank 3	Manager discretion.
Bank 4	No formal policy – manager's discretion.
Fin 1	Yes – but no details.
Assur 1	Formal policy – up to 5 days paid at manager's discretion.
Assur 6	Paid bereavement policy only.
Staff associations	
Insur 1	Formal policy up to five days for close relatives; others, one day.
Assur 2	Three days paid plus extra at manager's discretion.
Assur 3	Formal policy – three days paid with up to five at manager's discretion.
Assur 4	Discretionary. Usually two days paid and then make up out of holiday/flexitime.
Assur 5	Formal policy – but time and pay discretionary. May need to take from holidays/ flexitime.
No representation	
FM 1	Formal policy – up to five days paid.
FM 2	Discretionary.
FM 3	Three days paid can be extended at manager's discretion.
FM 4	Formal – up to five days paid at manager's discretion.
FM 5	No formal policy.

Table 7 Flexible working practices

Organisations providing these practices	
Part-time working	All
Flexible working hours	All except FM1 and FM5 (no representation)
Flexitime	All except Bank 2 and Fin 1 (trade unions); FM 1, FM 3, FM 4, FM 5 (no representation)
Job share	All except Insur 1 (staff association)
Term-time contracts	None except Fin 1 (trade union)
Full-time to part-time	All

It appears, then, that a range of flexible working practices were more commonly found within the finance sector organisations than were family-friendly policies that derive from the recent legislation. The patterns were consistent irrespective of the forms of employee representation that were available. One possible explanation is that there had been insufficient time for the legislatively supported FFPs to have been introduced at company level. A faster pace of implementation does appear to be associated with independent union presence (an interesting reversal perhaps of management's traditional claim that unions slow down organisational decision-making). This pattern is also evident in other analyses of surveys covering a range of industries and employers (e.g. Forth *et al.*, 1997).

An alternative explanation is that flexible working practices are more consistent with employer needs to provide increasingly continuous service facilities. These may be more easily achieved by retaining experienced staff through a combination of FWPs. Under these circumstances, it is not surprising perhaps that a number of the managers interviewed tended to think of family-friendly employment almost wholly in terms of temporal flexibility.

We now turn to the individual companies to review the implementation of FFPs and FWPs in more depth and in particular to examine the extent to which trade unions and staff associations have contributed towards the introduction of the different policies.

Rationale and establishment of FFPs and FWPs

As there do appear to be differences in implementation of FFPs, the same three-way classification framework is adopted for the Phase 1 micro-analysis; namely, establishments without formal employee representation; establishments that recognise a staff association; establishments that recognise independent trade unions. The establishments without formal representation tended to be small fund manager companies with a mean staff complement of 194 for their Scottish operations. The mean number of employees in Scotland for the staff association companies was 3,079 and 7,020 for the unionised companies. The proportion of women employees was slightly less than half in the fund manager companies and up to two-thirds in the staff association and unionised companies.

Non-union organisations

Interviews were conducted with management representatives in five organisations that had no formal arrangements for employee representation. A number of common themes emerged from these interviews.

First, the introduction of FFPs/FWPs was motivated largely by issues of labour competitiveness. As the HR managers from finance companies FM 1 and FM 4 stressed:

In Edinburgh, there is very, very high competition for staff and we have to make sure we retain the quality of staff. The way we can do that is by paying competitively, but also by having competitive terms and conditions and working environment.

(HR Manager, FM 1)

Current voluntary provisions are in place because of retention, not attraction. If you are flexible, you will retain people.

(HR Manager, FM 4)

Second, with management concerns for employee retention operating as a prime stimulus, it is not perhaps surprising that the family-friendly programmes in these organisations were primarily initiated and driven by management, without any formal employee involvement in developing the individual policies. Employee contributions emerged from individual requests or sometimes following staff attitude surveys.

Third, there were two main consequences of this management emphasis: the arrangements were largely informal, often without any written details and they were allocated to individual employees at the discretion of their line managers. For example, a senior manager at FM 5, when asked about formalisation of FFPs, commented:

> No – we have very few formal policies written on anything. In fact, the main policy is the contract.
>
> (Senior manager, FM 5)

Her counterpart at FM 2 explained that:

> We don't have a formal flexi-system but we do allow each department to run their own flexi-system so we will have certain people that take certain days off in lieu and things like that so they can work a wee bit flexibly. If they've clocked up extra hours they can take some time off if they need away early. The culture's very much, you know, 'if you take responsibility, we'll give you responsibility' … But, apart from women returners, we don't have many people generally working flexible hours on a regular basis.
>
> (Senior manager, FM 2)

At FM 3, the difficulties faced by staff (compounded by the somewhat patronising stance adopted by managers) were described by the Director of Personnel:

> Women returners usually ask for part-time and are often initially refused by the managers but work through it by negotiation. The women have to work pretty hard at convincing their managers but this is not a bad thing because then they are sure about what they want to do.
>
> (Director of Personnel, FM 3)

A fourth characteristic of these small organisations is that their:

> … traditional environment … has been largely driven by men [and] this sort of thing just isn't in their frame of reference.
>
> (Head of HR, FM 4)

Similarly, at FM 3, the Director of Personnel explained the reasons for not formalising the FFP agenda:

> [There is a] lack of female employees at the top. [They are] employed in lower-status jobs and the male-driven organisation means that formal policies have not been pursued so far.

The final point is that these small companies are sensitive to legislative and other external changes. Many have now recruited specialist HR managers, though often with little formal power, and these managers (often women) are trying to use combinations of legislation, formal benchmarking, informal soundings and social change arguments to convince their (male) superiors to adopt more progressive and embedded policies into these companies. However, as one Head of Personnel commented:

> It's evolving gradually. If you make quick change, people sort of back off.

Staff associations

Companies recognising staff associations (SAs) tended to be assurance-based. The somewhat conservative and staid image of assurance has changed dramatically in recent years as intense competitive pressures have forced most of the companies to attempt to expand their operations into other financial services such as mortgages. Some had merged or been taken over and others were engaged in demutualisation exercises. Most had opened up call-centre operations whilst reducing the number of branch outlets.

Nevertheless, vestiges of the 'old world' remained in their adherence to company-dependent in-house staff associations. It was also clear that progress on implementing universal coverage FFPs in the companies with SAs had not been rapid. However, compared to the informal approaches adopted in the non-union finance houses, it was apparent that more structured approaches were utilised to deal with employee issues. Many of the companies had established variants of staffing committees reporting to executive boards or other senior bodies. Nevertheless, SA membership on these committees was either on a minority basis for employees or was not represented at all. Hence, one company had a policy committee, composed of senior managers, which made the final decision on policies presented by the Staff Relations Department. Where employee SA representatives were present on committees, their influence was not palpably strong:

> Non-unionised but have a staff association and there is a consultative process rather than negotiation … Ultimately, if we don't agree, we can say 'we've consulted and we are going to do it anyway'.
> (Assistant General Manager Personnel, Assur 4)

Apart from the more structured approach to employment relations that might be expected

in large companies, similar constraints towards developing FFPs were identified as those noted for the non-unionised companies above. Indeed, in some cases, the culture seemed to be rather more resistant to change. In particular, the masculine ethos was identified as being especially pervasive by a number of HR specialists interviewed (see also Franks, 1999, p. 45). In discussing resistance to change the (female) staff relations specialist at Assur 2 pointed out:

> I think that can't be helped really, partly because, in common with an awful lot of other organisations, although the majority of people in the workforce are women, also the majority of women are at the bottom of the hierarchy and it tends to be men at the top.
> (Staff Relations Specialist, Assur 2)

A second potential obstacle to change was presented by the generally weak position of the HR function within the management hierarchy. Largely seen as an advisory body for line managers, the scope for many HR specialists to engineer strategic change appeared to be limited:

> The view is, I think, first and foremost we are here to run the business and it will be run by how the managers want to do it and Personnel should see them as our customer and what we can do to help them run the business the way they want to run rather than being an HR division that says 'if you don't do this, you won't be able to run your business'.
> (Staff Relations Specialist, Assur 2)

However, the issue of 'business needs' emphasised throughout the interviews provided opportunities for the human resources staff (and occasionally the staff association) to press for family-friendly arrangements. Recruitment and retention were identified by most respondents as pressure points for offering family-friendly concessions. As with the non-union group above, this was often undertaken in a pragmatic, individualised way, without codification, with the discretion of line managers providing the principal source of concessions granted. Benchmarking (and staff loss) were stated as the principal catalysts for drawing attention to changing terms and conditions.

Whilst voluntary FFPs were hard to find among these companies, flexible working patterns were common and, indeed, were treated by many companies as the embodiment of family friendliness, notwithstanding their introduction to serve the needs of the organisations. As one author noted:

> ... the word [flexibility] *has switched its meaning to describe the individual who is required to accommodate the demands of the workplace. So, whereas jobs used to be flexible, now it is people – the workforce who must be flexible.*
>
> (Franks, 1999, p. 75)

One additional feature of these companies in respect of FFPs is worthy of comment. Staff were encouraged when taking unexpected time off, for example, to look after a family member, to utilise a combination of available means. These could include any accumulated overtime, flexitime and holiday leave to combine with any discretionary leave offered by the company. At Assur 5, the HR Manager explained through an example how such a system operates in practice:

> *Somebody's son was off with chickenpox so they took time off to look after their son, then* [they] *immediately thought there is time off to look after your dependants. But my advice to*

> *the manager was: What was the situation? Was it an emergency? Was the child in an accident? And, if it had been a real emergency, we would probably give them paid time off, then a combination of holidays and flex time as the week progressed, but in that particular situation they used flex time to cover it.*
>
> (HR Manager, Assur 5)

Unionised companies

Details from seven unionised companies were available. These included four banks and three assurance/insurance companies. All were large organisations or part of major financial sector conglomerates. The recognised unions were MSF and Unifi and one TUC-recognised single-company union. One bank recognised both Unifi and a rather weak staff association and for this reason is covered in this section.

As with the non-union and staff association groups identified above, recruitment and retention along with meeting business needs for service provision have provided the major stimuli for adopting FFPs. At Bank 4, for example, the HR Manager commented:

> *...the most important reason for having FFPs is retention and attracting the best employees ... that's the whole business case. We're not going to chuck money away but, if people have been invested in for training, it makes sense to try and retain them.*
>
> (HR Manager, Bank 4)

In common with the SA and non-union companies, management discretion in dealing with employees and their requests was also evident. The differences were that, in unionised companies, there were joint forums established for unions to contribute to these issues. Also, at least to a modest extent, through these forums, the unions have been able to make an impression with their family-friendly agendas. The entitlements introduced tended to be codified and included in staff handbooks.

At Assur 1, for example, through concern for staff retention, the company established a joint working party (JWP) on the grounds that 'we have a very good relationship with the union ... they don't push for ridiculous agendas' (Staff Development Manager). Nevertheless, the company quickly established boundaries:

It was essentially about flexibility ... I don't think people were daft enough to think that we had a huge pot of money, things like a crèche, absolutely no. The union did not push for any of these other types of measures.

Notwithstanding the presence of the union, most of the agenda is:

... driven by HR from an employee relations standpoint although they do talk to them [unions] and allow them to throw their tuppence in and we'll take their views and see where we'll go from there.

(Staff Development Manager)

At Bank 1, where Unifi is recognised, it was again made clear that the company has been happy to work alongside the union:

Unifi (and prior to that BIFU) has had relations with the Bank a long, long time. It's a very long established relationship and a very amicable relationship as well.

(Employment Policy Manager)

Within that relationship, helped by legislative changes and competitive labour pressures, the union was in a position to exert some pressure on the company:

With parental leave, they [the union] were looking to have part of it paid and they were saying something about the CBI latest surveys that people were offering five days, but I can't find any evidence of that and what we've said is that it goes in as unpaid and we will review the take-up at the end of the year. If it's a very small take-up then maybe we will look at putting in some kind of financial incentive.

(Employment Policy Manager)

That the union can be effective was demonstrated in Bank 2 where the senior manager for employment policy commented that one of the outcomes of benchmarking was that:

... the unions will use it to ratchet you; if they get it at one bank then that's a tick in the box because they know they've got some leverage to get it at the other banks as well.

(Senior manager, Bank 2)

Management were also aware that the union (Unifi) would press, through the joint negotiating committee, for improved conditions. On parental leave for example:

We haven't fully rolled out our parental leave policy and I'm sure we'll get into a punch-up with the union when we come to do it because effectively the structure that we've drawn up is the basic legal minimum and obviously the aspiration will be to have something better than that.

(Senior manager, Bank 2)

At Bank 4, it was made clear by the manager interviewed that 'anything that is going to change substantially the way people work is bound to involve the unions'. Though, when asked whether issues like home-working would be negotiated, the reply was less positive for the unions: 'I think as a huge business case it will probably be consultative'. In other words, the decision would be essentially management determined with some union input into that decision, rather than jointly agreed through negotiation with the union.

In summary, it appears that unions, especially with market and legislative support, were able to raise family-friendly issues on to the agendas of consultative and other joint bodies. There was little evidence in this sector, however, of formal agreements based on joint negotiations between the parties. The tendency was for unions to raise or pursue a matter and for management to respond according to its priorities. There may be some fringe negotiations but the outcomes were still largely management determined. The next chapter looks at the unions' perspectives on their role in the provision of FFPs.

General employer perspectives

In addition to policy developments that were associated with the form of employee representation, managers also remarked upon a couple of relevant family-friendly issues that appear to be independent of representative arrangements.

It seems clear that the legislation has acted as a stimulus for many of the companies to review their family-friendly provisions. However, where companies had previously been offering conditions above the new legislative provisions, some were not progressing beyond these. They were arguing that they now meet the legislative requirements and cannot reasonably be expected to take further initiatives to restore differentials between their original provision and current statutory levels. As the management representative from one bank explained:

I think that my honest view would be if everybody was given the statutory minimum, we would give the statutory minimum. We would not be introducing unpaid parental leave if the statute did not require us to do it.

(Senior manager, Bank 3)

The second point connects to the extensive discretionary powers available to managers. A number of managers offered somewhat surprising perceptions of their employees. Weaving through several interviews arose a distinct feeling that employees are considered as essentially untrustworthy, unless refuted through long service without absence. For example, at one assurance company, the staff development manager interviewed was very concerned about the risk of abuse of time off for dependants, talking about 'punishing' people who use the entitlement 'too much', apparently even if the cause is genuine:

But, if someone, is, in our view, just using it too often, we will reserve the right to withdraw [payment].

At a bank, the manager expressed concern that different forms of paid leave can be abused by (and consequently might actually be withdrawn from):

... people who are going to abuse any sort of system that you operate so we've had quite a heated debate about whether we should replace the paid stuff that we already have with unpaid parental leave.

Summarising the companies' approaches

* Coverage of family-friendly employment policies appeared to be more extensive and formalised in companies that recognised trade unions but less so in companies with

in-house staff associations or without recognised representative forums. This finding confirms findings noted in large-scale surveys across a range of industries.

- Flexible working policies based on labour market demand were well established and more extensive than family-friendly arrangements.

- Management had considerable discretion in the determination and allocation of both family-friendly and flexible working policies.

- Organisational cultural factors such as a long-standing masculine ethos appeared to influence the coverage and/or application of at least some family-friendly policies.

3 | Union perspectives on family-friendly working

Clearly, there is a potential role for trade unions in promoting family-friendly working for employees through voluntary collective agreements with employers. At the same time, trade unions recognise the need both to attract new members and to demonstrate to existing members that they can offer services that promote their interests. Most employees are likely to have family or domestic commitments at some point in their life cycle.

From the company survey described in Chapter 2, it does appear that union presence was associated with a wider range of family-friendly policies; that these were likely to be codified; and that forums tended to be available in unionised companies for representative-based discussions on family–employment issues. Nevertheless, there were signs that the operational impact of these policies appears to be muted at the level of the workplace. This point is pursued in greater depth in the individual company case studies presented in Part II of this report. It is important therefore to examine union experiences of constraints or inhibitions on the implementation of family-friendly working within organisations. For these reasons, a number of telephone interviews were conducted at union head office level utilising a semi-structured questionnaire (see Appendix 1). Each respondent was asked background questions covering scope and trends of membership; union priorities and policies regarding FFPs; implementation and intervention roles in companies; and any constraints over their involvement with employers. Documentation relating to the union's approach towards family-friendly working was also requested in each case.

Of the seven unions interviewed, two were large, general finance sector unions and the remaining five were smaller, independent, TUC-affiliated, company-specific unions. In all cases, either the General Secretary or officer in charge of FFPs/equal opportunities was interviewed.

Union–management relations

On the whole, the unions agreed with the positive views expressed by the managers interviewed concerning union–manager relations. They reported satisfactory relations with the finance sector employers, ranging from formal partnership agreement in one case, through to 'very healthy' expressed by one union, 'fairly cooperative' by another and 'fairly good' informal relations by another. Three company-based unions indicated that they were involved in strategic decision-making within the companies. However, two unions reported mixed relations. One general union felt that their relationship 'could be improved', while a company-based union indicated that 'the company is schizophrenic' and supports partnership with the union 'as long as the union agrees with them'.

Union approaches to FFPs

Commitment

Six of the seven unions interviewed indicated that FFPs were part of their main union priorities, with one company-specific union indicating that it was their only priority at that time. The two general unions were engaged in explicit family-friendly campaigns, both policy directed at improving family-friendly leave arrangements through legislative reform. At the same time, these campaigns were also orientated towards increasing union membership. None of the smaller finance sector unions was involved in specific FFP campaigns, but the topic tended to be subsumed under an equal opportunities or, in one case, 'Dignity at Work' banner. Only one union indicated that FFPs were not a priority, simply because they had 'no hot topics at the moment'. However, this union had organised a formal union committee with the direct remit of negotiating for family-friendly arrangements with the company. Therefore, from this small sample, finance sector unions can be seen to be explicitly engaged with issues concerning their memberships' work–life balance.

Reasons for union interest

The unions' commitment to demonstrate their appreciation of the domestic pressures faced by members was explained in terms of membership demographics. The membership profiles of all the unions interviewed indicated a significant proportion of female members. In addition, for all these unions, membership growth was coming principally from among younger female workers (i.e. those most likely to have child-care commitments outside of work). However, the unions' desires to demonstrate their commitment to potential members' family responsibilities were less emphatic. While four of the seven unions were currently engaged in active recruitment campaigns, only one of the unions was explicitly using its FFP successes as part of its recruitment materials. Nevertheless, even for those unions that did not publicise their family-friendly agenda, FFPs were seen as important to potential recruits, since, in the words of one General Secretary of a company-based union: 'without family-friendly, people wouldn't join the union'.

Activity

All the unions indicated that they were pursuing family-friendly targets with employers at the time of the interview. While there was considerable variety among the respondents concerning their family-friendly agendas, a number of patterns were observable. Of principal note was an across-the-board concern with family-friendly leave arrangements, principally parental leave (five unions) and maternity leave (five unions). Other family-friendly leave arrangements targeted were time off for domestic emergencies (two unions), paternity leave (one) and time off for pre-adoption interviews and for anti-natal classes for fathers (one). The unions were also targeting flexible working practices, but to a lesser extent. Part-time working was a concern for three unions; while individual unions were addressing job-sharing arrangements; child-care provisions; term-time working and career breaks; and general concern with working hours.

Union perceptions of employer responses

While the unions considered this range of family-friendly targets as part of their agenda, their impressions of how the employers were reacting to union activities in these areas were less positive:

They get away with doing as little as possible.

(General union)

They don't think it's a priority and it's far from their main agenda.

(Company-based union)

However, in contrast to the views of the managers interviewed, a number of the unions indicated that their impact on formal family-friendly provisions had been significant. New agreements had been reached by two unions and existing arrangements extended in another case.

Despite their influence in formal provisions, all unions reported that there was a significant difference between union success in achieving these formal provisions and actual subsequent practice in the workplace:

Some policies are tokenistic.

(General union)

The policies are good – which is a start point for a cultural shift.

(Company-based union)

In principle very good, in practice not very good, [management] *talk ethical behaviour but it's the implementation of it. The root of the problem is cultural.*

(Company-based union)

Always a difference between policy and practice.

(Company-based union)

This picture appears to conform with the managers' reports of how they controlled and had discretion over family-friendly provisions in the workplace. Consequently, members' take-up of formal provisions was reportedly poor:

People don't take advantage of family-friendly policies.

(Company-based union)

Employees are unlikely to adopt [parental leave] *because it's unpaid.*

(Company-based union)

We have everything but no one does it. Take-up is incredibly low.

(Company-based union)

Union responses to management practice

Gaps between policy and practice resulted in a range of attempted union interventions over the practical application of FFPs in the workplace. All but one of the union officials reported that union interventions were the result of 'management attitudes':

The managers in the company are getting younger, are less experienced and are more results orientated. Therefore, lots of family-friendly issues revolve around poor management decisions.

(Company-based union)

Another single-company union official also concluded that union interventions had been required 'where a manager doesn't understand the spirit of the policy'. This perspective was supported by a general union respondent who felt there was a 'lack of sympathy on the part of managers'.

A number of family-friendly issues had been raised at union annual conferences and, more notably, a significant number of family-friendly associated cases had been taken to industrial tribunals. These cases tended to be concerned with flexible working practices and in particular with part-time or reduced hours working. One general union had taken up the case of maternity returners seeking reduced working hours, while separate cases pursued by three company-based unions were also associated with various aspects of part-timers' working terms and conditions.

Despite their problems in translating policy into practice, few of the unions provided their workplace representatives with training in family-friendly policies and provisions. Only one company-based union actively trained their representatives in the problems surrounding the implementation of family-friendly measures. Two unions provided FFP training for their full-time officers – for the rest of the unions, the input into family-friendly training for their representatives consisted of information contained in bargaining handbooks. Three unions felt that formal training was not necessary since the gender profiles of these unions (with a large number of female representatives) meant, in the words of one official, that the representatives were 'aware of family-friendly problems' and that a family-friendly sensibility 'goes with the turf'.

It appears from interviews with union officials that the finance sector unions are aware of members' domestic pressures and are committed to improving FFPs in the workplace. For some unions, however, as we saw above, the family-friendly agenda is tied up with gendered stereotypes and seen as principally a female issue. The unions all reported that their FFP activities had been positively received by their members:

More members are understanding their rights and asking us for assistance.
(General union)

However, this positive picture was complemented by expressions from two unions that this favourable reception to family-friendly policies by the membership was more passive than active:

Nobody can really be against it.
(Company-based union)

It would be more of an issue if it [FF] wasn't there – they expect it.
(Company-based union)

Interpretation of 'family-friendly policies'

Compounding the unions' approaches to training their representatives in the implementation of FFP was a total lack of formal interpretation of what constituted a family-friendly policy. While the managers interviewed in the company survey indicated that their interpretations were skewed towards flexible working, none of the unions reported a formal definition of family-friendly employment. However, the unions also considered flexible working to be family-friendly, since, for one general union respondent: 'That's what the membership want.'

This identification of FWPs with family friendliness raises the issue of whose language and meanings are being used in the workplace. Possible gaps between union and employers' interpretations of flexible working could account for the tensions between unions and managers concerning the implementation (or the 'spirit') of formal family-friendly provisions. While representatives of four unions indicated that there were no definitional problems associated with equating FWPs with FFPs, the remaining three unions expressed some difference of opinion with management over their definitions of FWPs:

It depends on levels of empowerment.
(Company-based union)

Group and trade union views are very different on the definition of flexible working.
(Company-based union)

Summarising union responses

- Unions were active in promoting extra-statutory FFPs and were reporting some successes.

- This success was to some extent negated by the uncertain commitment of companies in translating their policies into practice.

- Union success was also mitigated by management control of the implementation of these polices resulting in both a low take-up by employees and the necessity of union intervention over the application of FFPs.

- There was some evidence that family-friendly issues were perceived by some union officials to be more relevant to women union members or potential members than to men.

The survey phase of the study has been largely concerned with identifying factors that influence the formation of company policies for family-friendly employment and with examining the structures of emergent policies. From this phase of the study, a number of themes have been identified which will be further developed in Part II of the report which presents data from the four case studies.

Part II

Policy into practice

4 | Introduction to the second phase

A primary aim of the first phase was to seek insights into the nature of family-friendly and flexible working provision and the reasons, offered by management, for their adoption. The second phase looks in more detail at how these policies operate in practice.

We examine the level of provision, awareness, views and take-up of family-friendly and flexible working arrangements from the perspective of line managers, employee representatives and employees. We also describe the way in which company decision-making operates and explore the reasons for emergent patterns of policy operation.

The case study companies

Selection criteria

Four companies were selected from the first phase of the study for in-depth analysis. The original intention to choose six companies for close examination had to be revised as a consequence of intensified commercial activity in the financial services sector during 2000 and 2001. Whilst access was rarely denied, a number of organisations requested that we defer fieldwork owing to a combination of demutualisation exercises; restructuring; mergers or opposition to them; and acquisitions. The time constraints for the project required us to abandon those organisations that requested deferment. Nevertheless, as coverage of FFPs appears to be related to forms of employee representation, we were concerned to select at least one company from each of the main representative categories, namely: independent union recognition; in-house staff association; and no formal representative status. Two of our four companies recognised an in-house staff association, one recognised an independent

trade union and one had no formal representative arrangements.

Company profiles

Brief profiles of the four case studies are provided below. Pseudonyms are used for confidentiality reasons.

Castle Funds

Castle Funds is an established Edinburgh-based fund management company with £6.9 billion under management. It is a private limited company with over 80 per cent of the shares being owned by directors and staff. The core activity of the company is to provide a professional investment service for institutional, international and private investors.

Castle Funds employs 213 staff over two sites. Forty-seven per cent of employees are female and the average age is 33 years. The whole company was treated as a case study unit.

Formal approaches to employee involvement are minimal and consist of a communicative and consultative Staff Relations Committee. This body represents staff interests with a member from each operational area selected on a basis of volunteers and nominations.

Edinburgh Life Assurance Company

Edinburgh Life is an established assurance company managing over £78 billion. Its primary business is pensions but Edinburgh Life also provides insurance, savings and investments, and mortgages. Based in Edinburgh with operations in the UK and abroad, the Edinburgh Life Group employs 12,000 staff worldwide.

The case study unit is the group head office, which has 1,800 staff on one site. The core activity is the processing of customer claims, mostly for pensions. Fifty-seven per cent of employees are female and the average age is 33 years.

Edinburgh Life has an in-house, non-TUC-affiliated staff association (Edinburgh Life Staff Association, ELSA). All staff members are automatically members and representatives are selected through elections. Local representatives receive a modest time allowance to conduct their staff representative duties.

E-Bank

E-Bank is a wholly owned subsidiary of Edinburgh Life. This retail tele-bank was set up in 1998 and provides its 360,000 customers with the usual retail bank services online and over the phone. About 18 months ago, restructuring was accompanied by a new senior management team. E-Bank employs 1,200 staff, mainly in Scotland.

The case study unit is the head office based in Edinburgh and houses 1,066 staff. The core activity is to act as a call centre and to provide customer account administration. Fifty-seven per cent of staff are female and the average age is 29 years.

The staff at E-Bank have the same representative arrangements as Edinburgh Life, i.e. ELSA, although the two associations act independently of one another.

North Bank

North Bank plc is a retail bank with approximately 800 branches in its network servicing 20 million customers in the UK. It converted from building society status in 1997. North Bank employs 37,000 staff in the UK (the head office is in England) with 1,250 of those based in Scotland.

The case study unit comprises nine Scottish branches and two administration centres in Edinburgh and Glasgow. Eighty-two per cent of staff in the Scotland region are female. The average age is 33.

North Bank recognises one TUC-affiliated, company-based union with around four-fifths of employees being members. The union jointly negotiates with management on conditions and salaries.

Methodology

The research team aimed to obtain the views of four main groups in the decision-making process, namely line managers, employee representatives, human resource managers and employees. Interviews were used to target the first three groups and self-completion, questionnaire-based surveys of employees were conducted. Relevant documentation such as staff handbooks, formal agreements and organisational statistics were also collected using company and web-based sources of data.

Interviews

A common-core, semi-structured interview schedule was developed for managers, employee representatives and HR managers. Unstructured follow-up interviews with HR managers were also conducted where clarification was necessary. Notes were taken during these interviews, therefore quotes are from scribed notes and not audio recordings.

Table 8 shows the number of formal interviews conducted with different personnel in each of the companies.

Employee surveys

Self-completion questionnaires were distributed to a total of 1,118 staff in the four companies producing 533 usable responses, representing an overall response rate of 48 per cent. Distribution was random, although we ensured that copies were received by staff in departments where research team members had interviewed a manager. At Castle Funds, because of the small size of the organisation, the entire staff were surveyed.

The individual response rates for each company are shown in Table 9.

Table 8 Formal interview respondents

	Line managers	HR managers	Equal opportunities managers	Employee representatives
Castle Funds	7	2	–	3
Edinburgh Life	8	2	–	4
E-Bank	9	2	–	4
North Bank	9	1	1	5

Table 9 Survey response rates for the four companies

	Distributed	Returned	Response rate (%)
Castle Funds	213	119	56
Edinburgh Life	300	181	60
E-Bank	300	160	53
North Bank	305	73	24 *
Total	1,118	533	48

*The lower response rate at North Bank can be attributed to a less effective distribution strategy. At the other organisations, researchers were able to personally hand out questionnaires to individuals who then returned their sealed responses via the internal mail system. At North Bank, because of the branch network and security issues, line managers were relied upon for distribution and employees were asked to post returns.

5 | Policy provision, communication and awareness

In this chapter, the processes of policy development and the levels of provision in each of the case study organisations are described. The ways by which formal polices are communicated to line managers who are responsible for their operation are explored. Are managers given any training and support in decisions related to family-friendly policies? Are they aware of what the company provides? A summary of each company's approach to FFP provision is shown in Appendix 2.

The development and introduction of policies

Policy development at Castle Funds was ad hoc; there were no codified policies or staff handbook until 1998. Policies were often introduced in order to retain a particular individual, setting a precedent for the organisation. The HR Department was solely responsible for developing policies. Draft policies were taken to the Staff Relations Committee for feedback, although the HR Manager believed that the decision to introduce a policy was usually cost-driven unless required by law.

The policy strategy, including a current project on Work–Life Balance, for the whole Edinburgh Life Group was developed centrally by a large HR Department. Policy proposals were taken to a committee for consultation with business managers and the staff association, ELSA. Policies were then passed over to the subsidiaries, including E-Bank, for approval by their policy committee. Policy content at E-Bank was therefore essentially the same; the main difference being that, unlike Edinburgh Life, E-Bank did not have a flexitime system.

At North Bank, the Personnel Department at the head office in England drafted policies

which were first taken to business managers and then to the union for negotiation. The views of union members were canvassed if it was considered to be a 'big' issue or where there was no agreement between the parties. Personnel rolled out policies to all business units and branches across the UK.

We asked all interviewees why they thought their company had family-friendly policies. One common thread was the need to recruit staff in a competitive labour market:

> They are very aware of the image of the company. They want to be seen as a fair company and a fair employer ... to make sure that people want to come and work for us.
>
> (North Bank Training Manager)

Another common perception was that FFPs could help with staff recruitment and retention through improved morale, loyalty and commitment:

> They appreciate that you get the best from your staff if you treat them well ... Finance companies are good at this because there is a lot of competition in the labour market and you have to attract staff.
>
> (Castle Funds IT Manager)

In all four companies, there was a sense that these policies were also being provided because it was the 'right' thing to do. In Edinburgh Life and Castle Funds in particular, the provision of family-friendly policies was attributed to the company's 'paternalistic' culture.

This reason for having FFPs was much more commonly cited than legal compliance, which was mentioned by only a handful of interviewees across the four companies. However, as one North Bank union representative points out, the employee welfare ideal was not always borne out in practice:

> ... there is a genuine wish within group Personnel to provide a good working environment. It's not just about meeting legal requirements but the message gets diluted because of competing pressures.
>
> (North Bank union representative)

How 'family-friendly' messages were diluted by the processes of communication and operation is examined later in greater depth. First, we look at the formal provision in place in each of the companies.

Formal policy provision

Table 10 details the statutory minimum for these working arrangements alongside the level of formal provision offered by each company as stated in the staff handbooks. A range of potential flexible working arrangements are also shown.

A number of important points can be drawn from the table:

- In all four companies, elements of formal family-friendly provisions go beyond minimum statutory requirements.

- A similar pattern of coverage to Phase 1 was evident with the union-recognised company (North Bank) offering the widest formal coverage and Castle Funds, without any formal involvement arrangements, offering the least.

- In a number of areas of entitlement, managerial discretion was 'built in' to the formal provision.

Communication

In this section, we examine how these formal family-friendly policies were communicated to the line managers who were responsible for their operation.

Information

The main way in which policies were communicated across all four companies was via the staff handbook, either in paper-based or electronic format. Additional policies and amendments were circulated via email. However, at E-Bank, this communication went only to line managers whose responsibility it was to ensure that the rest of their team were informed. At North Bank, 'joint bulletins', agreed between the union and management, were widely distributed.

Edinburgh Life, E-Bank and North Bank provided line managers with a 'policy and procedures' manual which provided guidance on the intention of policies rather than the specifics of their operation. In Edinburgh Life, line managers also received advanced written notification about changes to policies. At North Bank, regional workshops were held for managers on equal opportunities, although not specifically covering family-friendly policies. At Castle Funds, managers did not receive any special documents or communications about these policies.

One E-Bank manager commented on the effectiveness of policy communication:

> Policies exist, but not everybody is aware of them. This is partly to do with communication, but also some of these things are of less interest to some people ... Communication is difficult in such a big company and so we tend to use email, but people can easily ignore this.
>
> (E-Bank Savings Manager)

Table 10 Voluntary provision offered by organisations compared to statutory entitlement

	Statutory entitlement in 2000	Castle Funds	Edinburgh Life Assurance	E-Bank	North Bank
Parental leave	13 weeks unpaid for children under five born on or after 15 December 1999	No mention in hand-book but statutory available	Extended age limit of child to eight years and lifted 15 December 1999 restriction	Extended age limit of child to eight years and lifted 15 December 1999 restriction	Statutory
Time Off for Dependants (TOFD)	Right to take reasonable time off to deal with an emergency involving a dependant. Unpaid	Covered by 'compassionate leave' policy	As statutory. managers may exercise discretion to authorise pay in some circumstances	As statutory. managers may exercise discretion to authorise pay in some circumstances	Initially paid leave or adjustment to working day. Further leave and pay is at manager's discretion
Paternity leave	None, although implied right under TOFD	Five days paid	Five days paid	Five days paid	Five days paid
Compassionate leave	None	Three days paid with 'special leave' at the manager's discretion given in 'exceptional circumstances'	Up to four days paid. with additional paid days at manager's discretion	Up to four days paid. with additional paid days at manager's discretion	Variable pay depending on circumstances
Flexitime	None	No	Head Office only, discretionary, subject to business needs	No	No
Informal flexibility of hours	None	No	No	No	No

Table 10 Voluntary provision offered by organisations compared to statutory entitlement (continued)

	Statutory entitlement in 2000	Castle Funds	Edinburgh Life Assurance	E-Bank	North Bank
Job sharing	None	No	Yes	Yes	Yes
Changing contracted hours	None	No	Returning part-time from maternity leave	Returning part-time from maternity leave	Policy for changing hours dependent on business needs Returning part-time/job share from maternity leave
Career break	None	No	Yes, unpaid	Yes, unpaid	Yes, unpaid
Term-time contracts	None	No	No	No	No
Home working	None	No	No	No	No
Phased return from maternity leave	None	No	No	No	No

Source: staff handbooks.

Support

Generally, across all companies, line managers consulted Personnel about non-routine matters, especially when disciplinary or grievance issues arose.

> I would consult Personnel if there was a serious issue ... but not for a more routine emergency.
>
> (Castle Funds Finance Manager)

> ... much of the day-to-day decision-making can be made by ourselves ... Personnel are there for a sounding board, for example, if it's an unusual case, or for help with the interpretation of the manual.
>
> (North Bank Branch Manager)

The relationship between line managers and HR was generally viewed positively by both parties in all four companies. At Castle Funds, all the managers and HR thought they worked well together. At North Bank, although on the whole managers had a positive impression of their relationship with HR, a few managers indicated that the level of service provided by HR depended on the HR adviser dealing with the matter, which could be different for each consultation. At E-Bank, managers commented that the practice of having an HR specialist assigned to their department was very useful:

> There are people appointed to our department so you build a relationship with them because of the amount of time you have to deal with them.
>
> (E-Bank Team Manager)

At Edinburgh Life, the 'relationship' between line managers and HR was not as strong:

> There is no relationship because you don't know who they are ... they are helpful when you do contact them though.
>
> (Edinburgh Life Customer Service Manager)

> Certain functions are helpful, some are very distant. Staff Relations can be helpful in certain situations but other times it is all very bureaucratic which is frustrating ... a common problem in big organisations.
>
> (Edinburgh Life Customer Service Manager)

Training

Line managers in the four case study companies were asked if they had received any training in addition to the initial communication of family-friendly policies. At Castle Funds and Edinburgh Life, line managers reported that no specific training was given at all. In the other two organisations, where training was provided, coverage was patchy.

At E-Bank, two line managers said they had been given a half-day training on family-friendly policies but the others stated that they had not received any form of training. The HR representative was aware that the training programme had not reached all of its target audience and explained why:

> I put it to the senior managers that I personally should go out and train managers on the family-friendly suite of policies but they didn't go for that because it would take up too much of my time. Instead, I had to train a couple of people who would then go out into the departments and train one person there and they would communicate it to the whole department but I'm not convinced that it was done thoroughly by everyone because I haven't had feedback from all the departments.
>
> (E-Bank HR Manager)

According to the Equal Opportunities Manager based at the North Bank headquarters, there were several ways in which training was given on the implementation and operation of family-friendly policies offered by the company; for example, workshops, online training, regional road-shows, staff booklets and flyers, bulletins and focus groups. Four managers said they had received training on flexible working, albeit one of them 'seven years ago'. When managers first took up a managerial post, they were given training which included management of people but in the words of one:

There's no refresher programme. We get bulletins, regional workshops. It is the responsibility of you as a manager to keep up to speed.

(North Bank Manager)

None of the managers interviewed reported receiving specific training on family-friendly policies. One branch manager identified that this lack of training contributed to the problem of inconsistent operation:

There is a wide variation in how these policies are implemented because there is no training in this at all and no HR involvement.

(North Bank Branch Manager)

Awareness

Line managers were asked whether a variety of family leave and flexible working practices were available at their workplace and whether this was on a formal or informal basis.

Table 11 represents each of the manager's responses concerning their awareness of statutory entitlements and company provision.

A number of features were prominent from these findings on managers' understanding and awareness of family-friendly policies and flexible working practices.

The highest levels of awareness were found for career break, paternity and compassionate leave. These policies, where available, were all formal with clear entitlements (although compassionate leave tends to have an *additional* discretionary element) and pre-date the Employment Relations Act 1999. This suggests that awareness is better where policies are codified and have been in place for some time. Awareness of the availability of flexible working practices was especially variable, but better in North Bank where they had a formal 'flexible working' policy in their handbook.

There was a wide range of responses with regard to statutory provisions. For example, at Castle Funds, there were four different responses from seven managers as to the availability of parental leave. At Edinburgh Life, three out of seven managers were confused about the same issue. During the interviews, it was clear that many managers were confused over terminology, often mistaking paternity for parental leave.

Managers' apparently limited awareness and confusion over policies demonstrates that communication and training strategies were not effective or, in some cases, not being used. Despite this apparent lack of organisational support, managers were expected to exercise considerable discretion in the operation of these policies. The ways in which managers took these decisions and the constraints they experience are considered in the next chapter.

Summarising policy provision, communication and awareness

- Managerial discretion was 'built in' to a number of formal provisions.

- Managers' main source of information on policies was the staff handbook.

- Limited training on FFPs was provided.

- Managers normally only consulted HR about extra-ordinary matters and overall viewed their relationship with HR positively.

- Awareness of policies was patchy and confusion over terminology evident, although awareness was better where policies were clearly codified and had been in place for some time.

- Awareness of statutory provisions was variable.

Table 11 Managers' awareness of family-friendly policies

	Castle Funds	Edinburgh Life	E-Bank	North Bank
Time off for domestic emergencies	******	✓✓****	✓✓✓✓✓**	A✓✓✓✓**
Parental leave	✓✓✓*X??	✓✓✓✓???	✓✓✓✓✓✓?	✓✓✓✓✓✓?
Paternity leave	✓✓✓✓✓*	✓✓✓✓✓✓	✓✓✓✓✓✓	AA✓✓✓✓
Compassionate leave	✓✓✓✓✓✓	✓✓✓✓✓✓*	✓✓✓✓✓✓✓	A✓✓✓✓✓✓
Career break	*XXXXXX	✓✓✓✓✓✓	A✓✓✓✓✓?	A✓✓✓✓✓✓
Flexitime	*XXXX	✓✓✓✓✓✓	XXXXXXXX	XXXXXXXXX
Flexibility of working hours	**	A✓***	AA***X?	AA✓**
Term-time working	XXXXXXX	A✓XXXX?	A✓XXXX??	AAAAXXXX
Home working	*****XX	****X?	*****XXX	*****XXXX
Changing contracted hours	✓******	AAA✓✓✓✓	AAA✓✓***	AAAAAAAA
Phased return from maternity leave	******?	✓******X	AA***XX??	A*****X??
N of managers	7	8	8	9

Source: line manager interviews.

Key:

A Available (not specified whether formally or informally)

✓ Available formally

* Available informally

X Not available

? Don't know/confused

Note: If no answer to a particular question was given by a line manager, no response was recorded.

6 | Managerial decision-making

Given that, in all four companies, the operation of many policies was left partly or entirely to the discretion of line managers, we were interested to find out what the pressures, constraints and criteria were that influenced those decisions. Using evidence from line manager and HR interviews, this chapter examines pressures to be both fair *and* consistent, job-based constraints and the decision-making criteria employed.

Formality versus discretion

Affording line managers the discretion to deal with individual cases within a basic framework of entitlements was a deliberate policy strategy. There are two reasons for this approach. First, each employee's needs at the time of taking emergency or compassionate leave will be different and legislating for all eventualities is impossible. From a company perspective, a line manager is well placed to make a judgement on an individual's needs because they know the employee and their circumstances and can tailor an appropriate response. Second, as a manager of resources, the line manager should have the authority to reject certain requests where the business operations for which he/she is responsible would be jeopardised.

The individualisation of a decision by the exercising of discretion can result in a positive outcome for an individual but it can also mean that consistency is sacrificed. This tension between treating employees 'justly', by taking into account their circumstances, and treating them 'equally', by adhering to formal policies, was recognised by managers in all four companies.

Managers at Edinburgh Life and North Bank viewed this tension as being part of organisational life and seemed to accept the consequences of treating employees differently.

They recognised the need for a minimum framework but were comfortable exercising their discretion within that. Managers at these two organisations were the most 'creative' in finding alternatives to formal policies. For example, some used other working time practices such as flexitime, holidays or a change to the working day in order to accommodate requests for time off for domestic reasons (see section on 'Time off for domestic emergencies' in Chapter 8).

At Castle Funds, the company with the lowest level of formalisation, managers were confident that the high level of discretion they enjoyed was the right approach. However, they were a lot less relaxed about the downside of discretion, often stating that they were worried that their decisions might 'set a precedent' and encourage other employees to seek the same treatment. This attitude can be explained by the fact that some policies had in fact been introduced through this route (see section on 'The development and introduction of policies' in Chapter 5). Most managers here felt that formalisation would result in family leave being regarded as an 'entitlement' leading to abuse by employees who might use it for other purposes.

Unlike the other companies where a concept of 'individualised fairness' was the focus, at E-Bank, consistency was the primary aim of the managerial decision-making process. Managers here were in a difficult position. Staff who felt they had been treated unfairly would compare themselves to other E-Bank staff and to staff at Edinburgh Life where, according to the HR manager, the tendency was to be more 'generous'. She offered this explanation:

It is a lot more cut-throat and fast paced over here. Also our managers are very inexperienced. Eighty per cent of our team leaders have less than one year's experience because they have come up through the ranks. They are not very comfortable with exercising their discretion. They like things to be in black and white and find it difficult to take decisions in grey areas.

(E-Bank HR Manager)

Nature of the job

Managers are constrained in their decision-making by the needs of business and in particular by the nature of the employee's job. There are two main ways that job-based constraints can be manifested: the ease with which an employee's skills can be substituted and whether or not the task is time critical. In addition, the working hours culture of the organisation will influence the decision-making process.

Substitutability

When an employee makes a request to be away from the workplace, for whatever length of time, the manager has to consider how their work will get done. If it is work that cannot be put off until their return then the question is 'Who will do the work?' The ease of employee substitutability is dependent on the number of employees in the organisation who are able to carry out the tasks normally carried out by the employee. This presents a particular dilemma for small companies and those who rely heavily on the specialist skills of individuals.

Edinburgh Life has a large workforce made up of customer service representatives possessing largely generic skills. Managers considered this to be a benefit when an employee wanted to change their working pattern, for example switching to part-time. Requests were usually accommodated by redistributing work or recruiting either

internally or externally. On a rare occasion where a request could not be accommodated, the employee was moved to another department with a vacancy and the company as a whole gained through retention. An internal vacancy system helped with this process.

Like Edinburgh Life, E-Bank has a large workforce made up of customer service advisers with generic skills. Managers there considered this high substitutability as an advantage when dealing with family-based issues such as maternity and parental leave. They emphasised the benefits of being able to plan for the replacement of the employee's skills.

Obviously, if people are off on maternity or parental leave, that has an impact on the ability to provide customer service so you have to plan for it. With a call centre our size [+400 staff], *the small amount of people involved means that it is only a minor itch, we tend to be able to cover.*

(E-Bank manager)

Generally, the staff at North Bank are substitutable in terms of their skills but the small number of staff available within each branch, compared to the large numbers on site at Edinburgh Life and E-Bank, meant that substitutability is a problem. While all the managers recognised that flexible working and family leave were a 'good' thing, they felt that these did not sit well with what they were being asked to achieve in the business given the tight staff complements they had to achieve it. This was felt particularly strongly in smaller branch units where staff levels were often at the minimum required for security purposes.

They make these decisions to introduce things for the right reasons but I feel that it conflicts with what we're asked to achieve in the business. On the one hand, you give people entitlements but, say someone is off on long-term sick, the targets don't change and that puts stress on other staff.

(North Bank Branch Manager)

You cannot operate FFPs if you don't have a sufficient core of staff to do the business.

(North Bank Branch Manager)

Managers perceived that the high work load coupled with tight resources meant that, when a staff member did go off for family reasons, the effects were felt by other employees. In the words of one manager: 'Absence makes the friends work harder.' He believed that this may contribute to feelings of resentment among staff without family responsibilities who felt that employees with families were receiving special treatment. The only evidence we found of this resentment related to employees with families getting priority with booking time off during school holidays when in fact the system was supposed to run on a 'first-come, first-served' basis.

At Castle Funds, the potential for staff substitutability was low. It is a small workforce with a high proportion of professionals with specialised skills and close relationships with their customers. In contrast to E-Bank, one Castle Funds manager found maternity leave very difficult to plan for:

I had two out of five in a team on maternity leave one after the other; one was the HoD, the other her deputy. Temps are difficult enough to find without finding managerial temps. We trained up someone else in the team and promoted her but then of course we had to demote her; eventually the deputy left and she got promoted again. The only way is

to have spare capacity and you can't do that in the competitive environment.

(Castle Funds manager)

Looking at the other three case studies, managers organising teams of professionals like legal advisers or IT specialists demonstrated views more closely aligned with managers at Castle Funds than those within their own organisation. Among these more specialised occupations, operating family leave and flexible working practices were perceived by their managers to be much more of a problem because of low employee substitutability.

The time factor

One way employees can manage their non-work commitments is by exercising some degree of control over when they are at their workplace. The level of working hours flexibility that a manager can allow, either informally or through a formal flexitime system, is dependent on whether or not the work task is time critical.

Edinburgh Life was the only company that had a formal flexitime system. As staff mostly did non-customer-facing processing tasks, managers had more control over the pace of work. This flexitime scheme consisted of staff having flexibility around start and finish times outside specified 'core hours' and were able to build up time credits to take off at a later date. Monitoring of the scheme was through a clocking in/out system. One manager had experienced trying to run the call centre department while all the staff were on flexitime. She found that the system that allowed staff to determine the start and finish time on a day-to-day basis was not compatible with the time-critical operations. Rather than get rid of the scheme altogether, they modified it so staff had to 'book' their flexitime, creating a shift system that did not cause problems as there were always people who wanted to start early and finish late. In addition, they merged staff into larger teams so there was a range of people in each team able to cover.

At E-Bank, staff carrying out back office functions were able to manage their work load. However, in the call centre, operations were dictated by customer demand.

We have shifts to fit our operational needs and, if someone is due to start on the phones at 10.00, then we really need them to be there at 10.00.

(E-Bank Call Centre Department Manager)

A previous management regime at E-Bank believed that any flexibility of working hours would be operationally impossible. The new management wanted to move away from this rigidity and create a hybrid system where staff could book time around core hours. There was also a formal shift-swap system where changes were agreed with the resource team of a particular area to make sure that the people who were swapping had the same skills set.

In the branch network of North Bank, the managers of customer-facing staff had similar views to those of call centre managers at E-Bank:

... there are some jobs which dictate a fixed pattern of working. There is a limit to how flexible you can be not only because of covering customer demand but because of security issues.

(North Bank Branch Manager)

Occasionally, staff were able to exercise some informal flexibility. If cover was available, which was more likely in a larger branch, they might be able to start later or make time up.

At Castle Funds, the Staff Relations Committee had requested flexitime. However, the request was rejected by the board. No firm reason was given other than that it would be difficult to manage and that they preferred the current system of informal flexibility to continue:

Some staff would like us to be more flexible than we are ... For example IT. They need to cover all workable hours so you can't have everyone coming in at 12.00 as the job doesn't support it.

(Castle Funds Director)

Practically [flexitime] *might be difficult so it is better to stick to the informal flexibility which we have in our department ... in other departments, they are more at the mercy of their manager. They've got different practices because they've got to get things done within stricter time scales. In our department, it doesn't matter when we do it as long as it gets done.*

(Castle Funds IT Manager)

The preference for informal flexibility of working hours by managers was a reflection of the attitude that, despite frequently stating that there was a high degree of manager/employee trust, managers, who were seemingly ignorant of the provision of 'core hours' within a flexitime system, believed that if any form of formal flexitime were introduced employees would abuse it by coming in at inappropriate times.

Working hours culture

While not the main focus of this research, a long working hours culture in an organisation has clear implications for 'family-friendly' employment; the longer parents are in the workplace, the less they are with their families. However, as discussed later in this chapter in the section on 'Managers' perceptions of employee input', access to leave and flexible working arrangements is often determined by the manager's perceptions of the employee's input in terms of the time spent in the workplace. Therefore, we will briefly examine the working hours cultures in the four case study companies, first, among all employees and, second, among managers. Table 12 compares the nature of overtime in the companies.

The standard employment contract at Castle Funds stated that the normal working week was 35 hours, from 9.00 a.m. to 5.00 p.m., Monday to Friday. Overtime may be required of staff because of the 'particular needs of the business' and payment was only allowable for staff below head of department level (source: Castle Funds staff handbook). Staff at Castle Funds worked the longest hours out of the four companies and were the least likely to be compensated. Although non-managerial employees were entitled to claim for extra hours, one stated that she did not feel comfortable claiming for the extra hours because her boss worked many more hours.

Some managers at Castle considered long working hours to be a matter of choice resulting from individuals being 'very self-actualising'. However, long hours can have adverse effects on other employees and were perceived by many as being unnecessary:

I am concerned that it is still part of the firm's culture to praise additional commitment of time in the knowledge that this must be at the expense of family relationships.

(Castle Funds Investment Manager)

I think people stay too long and we have a culture in some areas where, if you don't work long hours, you are not seen as a good worker. The culture here would have to

Table 12 The nature of overtime				
	Castle Funds	Edinburgh Life	E-Bank	North Bank
Average overtime hours worked per week: all employees	7	3	2	5
% working 10 hours or over overtime per week: all employees	28	10	2	18
Average overtime hours worked per week: managers	10	6	5	5
% not compensated for overtime hours: all employees who performed overtime	54	5	6	8
Most common reason for working overtime: all employees who performed overtime	'To get all my work done'	'I need the money'	'I need the money'	'To get all my work done'
N	116	169	160	72

Source: Staff surveys.

change for flexitime to work ... I tried to start leaving at 5.00 but my colleagues would look at their watches and I didn't feel comfortable. People are valued on how long they stay at their desks. They are not task orientated.

(Castle Funds HR Manager)

At Edinburgh Life, staff worked a 35-hour week and, in the case study unit, most staff made use of the formal flexitime scheme (see Table 17 in Chapter 8). There was also an overtime scheme applicable to most non-managerial grades at which overtime was paid at time-and-a-half. The average overtime hours per week for all employees was three hours. Generally, extra hours were worked because employees 'needed the money' and 94 per cent of those doing overtime were either paid (the majority) or took time off later.

E-Bank operated a 35-hour week, with many of the operational staff on a fixed shift system. Overtime worked on the same basis as at Edinburgh Life although staff could not build up time as there was no formal flexitime system. This organisation had the lowest reported level of overtime among staff of all the four companies and most of those who did work extra time were compensated. As with Edinburgh Life, overtime was largely done because employees needed the money.

When North Bank merged with another company, staff contracts were changed from 36 hours a week to 35 hours to be worked between 8.00 a.m. and 8.00 p.m. and to include alternative Saturday working and no time built in for setting up, tea breaks or cashing up at the end of the day. It is therefore not surprising that workload was the most common reason for doing overtime, indicating that there was some organisational pressure to work extra hours. The working hours problem was apparently recognised by senior management:

[The CE] is keen that staff aren't working long hours because he doesn't want to either. But this message has been diluted and staff still feel that they have to work the hours because they don't want to say no to management .... The CE addressed the union conference and, although the messages he was sending were very positive, he did show a lack of knowledge of the reality of the situation, both of the culture and of resources issues.

(North Bank union representative)

In all organisations, except North Bank, managers were working much longer hours than other employees (see Table 12 earlier in this chapter). Most managers above a team leader type role were employed on contracts where they had to work the 'hours required to do the job'. This was also found to be the case by Hogarth *et al.* (2000) whose study into work–life practices across Great Britain found that professional and managerial staff are more likely to be 'employed to fulfil responsibilities without reference to working time' (Hogarth *et al.*, 2000, p. 9). Overall, managers were accepting of the longer hours with many of them stating that 'it goes with the territory'. However, there was confusion over the degree to which long working hours were voluntary and heavy workloads were often mentioned:

Interviewer: *Are the long working hours people work a matter of choice?*

Manager: *A lot of the time yes. It's a blend of choice, having high standards, the pressure to get things done and being willing to take on responsibility. It is viewed favourably. They say to you that you're working too hard then they pile the projects on you.*

(Castle Funds Manager)

... if you don't do the hours you fall too far behind because I have so many responsibilities but I think every company is the same.

(North Bank Branch Manager)

I mean, what's the difference between working until 5.00 or 6.30, it will all be there in the morning anyway. I think I do it to try and make the next day easier but it rarely is. I think it is personal choice to a large degree. There is a workload issue but it has a lot to do with pride, proving that you can do it.

(E-Bank Call Centre Manager)

The nature of managerial contracts meant that there was no real concept of 'overtime' and extra pay specific to longer hours spent in the workplace was rare (also found in Hogarth *et al.*, 2000). However, there were other ways in which managers may be compensated for longer working hours.

Managers at Castle Funds were the most likely to feel compensated for the extra hours they work through higher salaries and bonuses. One manager believed:

The 35 hours is a standard contract but as people progress you get paid more so you give more.

At Edinburgh Life, managers thought that they were compensated through the bonus system or by taking days off. At E-Bank, a few managers felt that they were compensated through salary and bonuses but others did not feel compensated at all. At North Bank, only one manager thought that there was any compensation (through salary) for the extra hours worked.

Decision-making criteria

Notwithstanding the potential constraints outlined above, there were other criteria that fed into managerial decision-making processes. Perceptions of employee inputs and managerial attitudes to atypical working patterns were important influences on managerial decision-making.

Managers' perceptions of employee inputs

In all the companies, except Edinburgh Life, managerial perceptions of employee commitment were explicitly stated as an important factor in deciding the level of access to family-friendly policies. What constituted a 'good' employee could be measured in terms of the skills they possessed or their output. However, more often it was measured by the number of hours spent in the work place.

At both E-Bank and North Bank, perceptions of employee input were a consideration when deciding whether to exercise discretion in extending periods of paid leave.

If someone contributes well to the business, if they put in the hours for no extra pay, then that shows commitment and we'll go outside the policy for them. If someone just comes in from 9.00 to 5.00 and are not that bothered about being here then they are not going to get the benefits of the manager's discretion.

(E-Bank Mortgages Manager)

Some people are flexible and some aren't. [An example of] where flexibility tends to be one-sided, some staff won't work Saturdays because it's not in their contracts.

(North Bank Branch Manager)

At Castle Funds, this evaluation of employees was less of an influence on the decision to grant paid time off and more of a determinant of access to flexible working patterns. Informal flexibility of working hours was only available to individuals in high-level jobs. When an employee wanted to change his or her working patterns, the extent to which they were valued by the company was an important factor. For example, one senior investment manager was allowed considerable freedom and time off in order to pursue his career as an author in the field. Workplace flexibility was regarded as a reward for long working hours and acceptance of high stress levels.

Managers' attitudes to flexible working practices

When an employee wanted to reduce working hours because of personal circumstances, the manager's attitude to flexible working practices affected the outcome. Castle Funds and E-Bank had a high proportion of full-time workers (94 per cent and 93 per cent respectively) and were the least receptive to part-time working. In the case of Castle Funds, this stemmed from a belief that business objectives could be achieved only by staff being on traditional full-time hours. At E-Bank, a previous management regime held the same views and, although the new management fully recognised the benefits of flexible working, it was taking a while for attitudes to change.

The business benefits of flexible working were most strongly stated at the two retail banks where opening hours were long and the workload variable. At North Bank (62 per cent on full-time contracts), all the managers valued the fact that part-time workers covered lunches, evening shifts and weekends and filled in when they were short staffed.

From a call centre perspective it means we can match manpower levels with customer demand. At the moment because we have a lot of full-time staff we are over staffed in the

middle of the day. That is very demotivating for staff who have to sit around and wait for the calls to come in. Having part-time staff maximises efficiency and reduces costs.

(E-Bank Call Centre Manager)

Communication was a difficulty identified with managing employees on atypical hours. This was the most strongly felt at North Bank and E-Bank where managers may not see an employee for long periods of time. To overcome this, managers often voluntarily worked outside their normal pattern in order to have direct contact with employees. One branch manager at North Bank felt it important that he did this so those who worked outside traditional working hours did not feel alienated. Castle Funds was the only company where managers stated that they would refuse a request to work part-time purely on the basis that it would be too difficult to manage.

Whether or not a job was regarded as suitable for part-time or job share depended on the place the employee occupied in the hierarchy. Positions without a supervisory element were more likely to be approved in all four companies but the strength with which this applied varied. Managers at Castle Funds in particular strongly believed that managerial positions were not suitable for part-time working.

One woman here wanted to work three days a week, so she came up with the solution of changing her job to project work which is more suitable for part-time working, but her role as a manager was not suitable for part-time working. Managers have to be there for their staff all the time so she couldn't go part time.

(Castle Funds Director)

... it is the 'attitude' of the directors/managers which can make it difficult to take advantage or press for more flexible work patterns. You will not be seen as being as committed to your job and may suffer in terms of potential promotion and salary.

(Castle Funds Accountant)

Similar attitudes were found at E-Bank:

At clerical and supervisory level it would be a poor show if we couldn't cover that level, but it is more difficult to cover department manager level. The further up you go, it's harder to work part-time.

(E-Bank Mortgages Manager)

We are hoping to start a family in the next couple of years and I find myself worrying about my job prospects here as I have not seen any job share or part-time managers/ team leaders.

(E-Bank Customer Service Representative)

At Edinburgh Life and North Bank, flexible working appeared to be less of a barrier to career progression. At Edinburgh Life (87 per cent full-time staff), the HR Manager had worked a variety of flexible working patterns and there was a Customer Service Manager who was able to discharge her duties on a part-time basis. At North Bank, managerial job share was positively encouraged. However, it is worth noting that the job-sharing Branch Manager who we interviewed had to give up her position as a regional manager and take a demotion to branch manager level because job sharing was not considered appropriate for that level.

Summarising managerial decision-making

• Tension existed between formal policies and exercising informal discretionary practices that take into account individual circumstances.

• The more substitutable the employee in terms of both numbers and skills, the easier it was to manage FFPs.

• The ability of managers to offer flexibility of working hours was dependent on whether or not the task was time critical.

• Prior commitment of time by employees could influence discretionary access to FFPs.

• Managerial attitudes to flexible working influenced employee access to such practices.

7 | The role of employee participation

This chapter examines the extent of employee influence on workplace family-friendly employment policy decisions, the ways in which any influence is expressed (specifically individually or collectively) and the implications of these findings for the Government's promotion of voluntarily determined family-friendly arrangements that extend beyond statutory baselines.

The role of employee representatives

... at Castle Funds

On the whole, the consultative body, the Staff Relations Committee (SRC), exerted very little influence on decision-making. It had no family-friendly remit and no reported influence on adoption of family-friendly policies. While issues could be brought to the attention of senior management via the SRC, the policy decision rested with either the board or an operations committee. Neither of these groups had any Personnel or employee representation. The following interview quotes indicate the limits of SRC influence on the provision of family-friendly policies:

I don't think it's made any impression. The SRC, to be fair, have tried but nothing seems to come of it.

(Castle Funds Assistant Director)

They don't discuss that, they don't make decisions.

(Castle Funds IT Manager)

When FFPs are implemented it is 90 per cent of the time Personnel driven.

(Castle Funds Staff Relations Committee Member)

While the employee representatives reported that some FFPs had been introduced through 'consultation', they also stated that suggestions made by the SRC were only sometimes taken seriously by management. In the words of one manager, this lack of decision-making influence meant that:

... a lot of people see it [SRC] as a waste of time, especially if ideas keep getting knocked back.

Rather than a decision-making forum, the SRC was seen instead by managers as a communications mechanism with senior management, with the employee representatives serving as information channels. However, despite this reported role, employee representatives received no family-friendly policy training and, of the three representatives interviewed, only one was familiar with statutory FFPs.

Representative arrangements at Castle Funds did not appear to have had a significant impact on the family friendliness of employees' working lives. Policy level influence remained in the gift of senior management, while operational level influence was practically non-existent. No formal role for employee representatives in decisions made by line managers was cited concerning employee access to family leave or flexible working arrangements.

... at Edinburgh Life

Edinburgh Life shared a common ancestry with E-Bank, so the in-house representative body, ELSA, shared similar terms of reference and membership structure as the staff association body at E-Life. Nevertheless, the two management teams worked independently of one another, as did the two representative bodies. There were, however, bi-annual consultative meetings between group personnel and national representatives drawn from the pool of local representatives in each company. There were also cultural similarities between the two representative systems in that ELSA, based at Edinburgh Life, enjoyed the support of senior management and of human resource specialists and at least the tolerance of line managers. This support was reflected in the establishment of a 'partnership agreement' between Edinburgh Life and ELSA. One possible explanation of this support may arise from the perceived lack of influence provided by ELSA, a point emphasised by one of the elected representatives:

[ELSA] does not have a lot of influence, for example, no say over salaries. Smoking policies were relaxed on site because of ELSA. They may seem to be minor things, but they are the things which have a big impact on staff.

(ELSA representative)

Nevertheless, it was broadly acknowledged among representatives and managers that ELSA did have its positive uses, acting as a 'barometer of how things will be received by the staff' and for 'sharing information'. Management appreciated the value of the body for its ability to articulate employee opinion before this coalesced into an 'issue'. Both ELSA representatives and managers were united in their view that, whilst ELSA enjoyed no shared decision-making powers with management, they did have some input into the process of decision-making.

There was some evidence that both management and staff were inclined to support ELSA, of which staff automatically became members on joining the company, in preference to a trade union. In fact, at one point, staff were asked to vote if they wanted to keep ELSA as opposed to an external union and, in the words of one representative, the 'staff wanted to keep ELSA'. The same representative pointed out that, originally, senior management spearheaded ELSA. Subsequently, the General Manager 'went through a huge exercise to promote ELSA to increase awareness'. On being asked about the effects, in terms of relations between the company and ELSA, the representative replied:

Very good. It's the organisation's baby. It invented it and gave it to staff to use. It's not something staff were crying out for, but it was welcomed...We don't need a union to do stuff effectively.

(ELSA representative)

Whilst some antipathy towards the prospect of an independent union was evident, there was little obvious enthusiasm among constituents for ELSA either. According to one representative:

At the election, they were struggling to get nominations. I think it is a combination of staff not really bothered and lack of faith in ELSA. A lot of that is because of the time it takes to get things done. I only get one or two replies when I ask for comments. I can't blame people, though, I was a bit like that before I was directly involved.

(ELSA representative)

ELSA had played a part in bringing about change in terms of family-friendly employment though the enhanced coverage of parental leave for all children under eight and an increase in the provision for paternity leave from three to five days. However, according to one manager, the main reason that the number of days was increased 'was on the basis of managers operating their discretion'. For this same manager, even when success can be attributed to ELSA, it was only very partial:

I don't think things have been introduced because of ELSA. I think management would have introduced them anyway. ELSA is important for sharing information. It's shared up-down down-up, up to a point.

(E-Life Manager)

Representatives received very little training in their general responsibilities and none in dealing with family-friendly issues. Their operational role seemed limited to the occasional support of employees when disputing implementation of company policy or exercise of management discretion with their line managers. Nevertheless, these protective roles were carried out only rarely.

... at E-Bank

The input and influence of the representative body, ELSA, at the policy decision-making level at E-Bank appeared to be greater than that of the Staff Relations Committee at Castle Funds. According to staff representatives, ELSA had the support of the senior management, was 'supported wholeheartedly by the Executive', and Personnel was also reported to be 'very pro-ELSA'. As shown above, the situation at Castle was quite different, with the SRC largely marginalised by senior management.

However, ELSA was valued by management principally as a communications mechanism and not in a formal decision-making role. For managers, ELSA was used to sound out a policy that was to be widely broadcast to staff. The employee representatives also saw their role as one of information sharing, communications with staff, or even to 'canvass for management'

in the words of one representative. Despite consultation with E-Bank concerning new policies, ELSA had no official remit in organisational decision-making. However, it enjoyed some FFP successes: a database of those employees looking for job shares had been established on the back of an ELSA suggestion. Changes to shift patterns had been modified after consultation with ELSA and ELSA had brought up the issue of the entitlement of partners in same-sex couples to partner's benefits under the company pension scheme – which the company accepted as policy.

However, while these successes made it appear that ELSA had influence over the policies that were introduced, management's view was that:

... a lot of the time it is things that senior management would have done anyway.

(Call Centre Manager)

This view was also recognised by the employee representatives:

We can't change very much because we're not a union. We say how the staff are feeling and then it is up to the company whether they take it on board and what they do about it ... it is basically a management decision, we can give feedback but it is basically up to the manager.

(ELSA representative)

Therefore, while ELSA could raise issues with management, it had no formal influence to prevent these issues from being ignored:

We do push for things that we don't get, like child care. We have pushed for a crèche on the premises and they have refused, saying it is because of insurance.

(ELSA representative and Call Centre Team Manager)

The above issues indicate that the actual influence of the employee representative body over family-friendly decision-making at E-Bank was both informal and relatively weak: management controlled the agenda. It was clear that the representatives saw their role as one where they were not to 'cause waves' or to 'stir up trouble'.

Consequently, the employee representatives did not go beyond their information-sharing and advisory role:

> A father asked me recently if he might be able to get time off to go to pre-natal classes with his wife. I phoned Personnel for him and they said he would have to strike up a deal with his manager.
>
> (ELSA representative)

Therefore, while their informative role was emphasised, the paucity of decision-making influence exerted by ELSA at all levels meant that:

> ... nine times out of ten we can't actually help, we can just give advice – they have to go to their managers.
>
> (ELSA representative)

Given the consultative role earmarked for ELSA, the policy decision-making locus remained with senior management and the operational decision-making locus with line managers. Significantly, in contrast to ELSA's positive relations with senior management, the employee representatives and many of the line managers interviewed reported a distinctly different atmosphere between line managers and ELSA. This impacted on the influence of the employee representative agency at the operational level of family-friendly polices.

There was clear evidence of a certain amount of resentment among the line managers concerning the role and remit of ELSA. In particular, problems were reported with 'lower management because that is where the issues arise' since these line managers felt that ELSA was 'stepping on their toes'. Another employee representative reported that:

> Line managers find it difficult to deal with the time required by a rep. to do their ELSA duties ... you can't deal with someone who is upset in five minutes.
>
> (ELSA representative)

... at North Bank

The situation and influence of employee representation was considerably different at North Bank. Unlike the other case study companies, at the national level, the North Bank independent union had a formal input and influence over decision-making and was 'taken very seriously' by senior management. Yet, despite the union's formal input at policy level, human resource and line managers disagreed with the union representatives about its actual level of influence over policy. They maintained that the company only implemented those policies raised by the union that it would have done anyway. In the end, the 'company has driven most of the FFPs rather than being pushed into them by the union' (Equal Opportunities Manager). The impression of union influence was created because the:

> ... union only succeeds where the company lets it ... the company will go with the union when it suits them. The union is not as powerful as it might be.
>
> (Training Manager)

Even some of the employee representatives agreed with this view. One union representative reported that, at national level, the company would 'pretty much do everything to push what they want through'.

Despite the union's formal decision-making input and control, as with the other companies, the reported relationship between the union and line managers at North Bank painted a different picture at the operational level, with some employee representatives reporting a less positive experience:

At local level you are definitely looked on by management as an interference.

(Union representative)

... the union doesn't have the same teeth that it does at national level.

(Union representative)

At the operational end of family-friendly policy in particular, the influence of the union appeared to be significantly weaker. While, at national level, union decision-making input was formalised and with negotiating powers, at the local level, union representatives had no proactive decision-making role. Instead, their role was to inform members of their rights as and when members came to them with problems. These employee representatives, as at the other case study sites, had a largely information sharing and communications role at local level. However, both this local level informative role and higher level union influence over national policy were weakened by the attitude of the members who were described as both apathetic and fearful of rocking the boat.

On the one hand, the weakness of union influence was attributed to the membership's unwillingness to take action:

The staff won't strike therefore their [union] influence is not so great, so it's difficult for them to oppose things that management wants.

(North Bank Branch Manager)

People don't even vote. Everybody moans but when it comes down to it they won't do anything about it.

(North Bank Branch Manager)

However, the lack of action by the membership was also attributed to fear of confronting managers and a lack of job security among employees (and by default also among their representatives):

People are scared of conflict, particularly with the managers that they work with ... there is a problem of both awareness and confidence among staff.

(Union representative)

A lot of people will ask me for information and ask me not to do anything about it ... people don't want to rock the boat.

(Union representative)

Therefore, despite the signs of union influence at national level policy, issues of relative power distribution between employees, union representatives and their managers at branch level were having a significant impact on the operationalisation of family-friendly policies within North Bank.

This unwillingness of local representatives to confront management over issues had implications for the union's ability to represent its members effectively in the face of management resistance. In this respect, some employee representatives may have been unintentionally allowing family-friendly practice to diverge from union negotiated national policy. Consequently, even though formal family-friendly provisions at North Bank went beyond the statutory minimum, the influence of union negotiated policies at branch level was being diluted. This was the consequence of the membership's and employee representatives' reluctance or inability to engage in adversarial relations with management at North Bank.

Direct (individual) employee participation

Direct employee participation concerns employee perceptions over the extent and means by which they can individually contribute to organisational decision-making. The surveys of employees in the four case study companies examined their perspectives on different dimensions of employee influence. Respondents were asked to indicate their perceived levels of involvement in decision-making in the provision and practice of FFPs and flexible working practices in the organisations. They were also asked about their involvement in decision-making more generally.

Table 13 indicates that few respondents felt that they were able to make a difference to the sorts of family-friendly arrangements introduced in their organisation. However, there were marginal differences between the organisations. While 19 per cent of respondents at Castle Funds felt they were able to make a difference, only 8 per cent at

Edinburgh Life Assurance felt they could do this. At both E-Bank and North Bank, 12 per cent of survey respondents felt they could make a difference.

Over half the respondents across all organisations were of the opinion that: 'I am never asked my views about family-friendly working arrangements available in the workplace'. There were no appreciable differences between organisations.

Nevertheless, as Table 14 shows, around half of respondents across all the companies stated that managers were 'good' or 'very good' at both: 'Providing me with a chance to comment on proposed changes to the company' and: 'Responding to suggestions from employees'. There were no great differences between organisations on either of these measures. Compared with other questions about how good managers were at various behavioural tasks relating to employees, managers were perceived to perform less well at involving employees in decision-making across all companies.

Table 13 Proportion who 'agree' or 'strongly agree' with the following statements about how the company handles work–life issues

	Castle Funds	Edinburgh Life	E-Bank	North Bank
'I feel that I am able to make a difference to the sorts of family-friendly arrangements that are introduced here' (%)	19	8	12	12
'I am never asked my views about family-friendly working arrangement available at this workplace' (%)	53	61	50	60
N	118	178	160	73

Table 14 How good are managers at this workplace at the following?: proportions stating 'good' or 'very good'

	Castle Funds	Edinburgh Life	E-Bank	North Bank
'Providing me with a chance to comment on proposed changes to the company' (%)	53	49	53	56
'Responding to suggestions from employees' (%)	50	50	55	48
N	119	178	159	73

Summarising the role of employee participation

- Neither representative bodies nor individual employees were perceived to make a significant impact on company family-friendly employment strategies. Moreover, practice over implementing FFPs and FWPs appeared to be dominated by line manager discretion.

- The most substantial influence on the provision of FFPs was found in North Bank where there was a union. However, ELSA also had some success in extending family leave beyond the statutory minimum.

- Management, and even some employee representatives, considered that policies pushed for by representative bodies would have been adopted by management in any case.

- Positive relations were reported between senior management and the representative bodies although there was some evidence that lower level management did not share the same view.

- At operational levels, employee representatives worked mainly in an information-sharing and advisory capacity and had no role in the FFP decision-making process, which was the jurisdiction of the line managers.

- Over half of all respondents reported that they had never been asked their views on FFPs.

- Half of the respondents did feel they were consulted over company changes and employee suggestions.

8 | Employee experiences

In this chapter, we examine how the companies' policies and practices outlined in Chapters 5, 6 and 7 affect employees. Are employees aware of and taking up family-friendly policies? What affect does managerial discretion have on usage? Are there provisions that employees want to take but do not and why?

Communication and awareness

In order for employees to avail themselves of policies, they must first be aware that they exist. Chapter 5 showed that managers' awareness was limited. This section looks at the same issues among employees, uncovering broadly similar patterns.

Communication to employees

Employees were given information about FFPs in exactly the same way as managers, i.e. via the staff handbook in either paper-based or electronic format. We asked employees *who* was the single most important source of information. The results are shown in Table 15.

At Castle Funds, the Personnel Department was overwhelmingly the most important source of information with no other actor playing a

significant role. At Edinburgh Life, the Personnel Department was also the most important source. This department ran a help desk which answered queries from both staff and managers about company policies. At E-Bank, line managers played a more important role reflecting the fact that they were given specific responsibilities to ensure staff were informed about new or changed policies. At North Bank, too, line managers had responsibilities to inform staff about new and changed policies. Here, there was a notably less significant role for Personnel suggesting that staff in the branch network do not have much direct contact with HR. However, when asked to rate how good managers were at keeping staff informed about changes to company HR policies, North Bank managers scored the lowest with less than half of the respondents rating them as 'good or very good'.

Given that the purpose of employee representatives was viewed by management primarily as a communication channel (see Chapter 7), the results for their role as a source of policy information are disappointing. This held true for North Bank, which had procedures in place to ensure that all staff read

Table 15   Who is the most important source of information on FFPs?

	Castle Funds	Edinburgh Life	E-Bank	North Bank
Personnel Department (%)	83	37	32	14
Line manager (%)	4	26	37	36
Employee representative (%)	2	18	10	14
Co-workers (%)	6	12	14	18
Other (%)	1	3	3	5
No information provided (%)	4	4	4	13
N	112	163	149	61

Source: Staff surveys.

and signed joint bulletins on employment practices issued by the union and management. As with line managers, employee representatives in each organisation had not received family-friendly specific training, even after the introduction of new rights under the Employment Relations Act 1999. It would appear that, although representatives were viewed as a way of providing information and support for employees, they were being under-utilised for that purpose, and were not given the tools, through training, to do so.

Employee awareness of family leave

The results of the staff survey, shown in Table 16, revealed similar patterns of awareness as the line manager interviews (see section on 'Awareness' in Chapter 5). Employees across all four companies were most aware of the formal policies that were paid, i.e. compassionate and paternity leave. Awareness of time off for domestic emergencies was not particularly good, although for dependants it is a statutory right (albeit a relatively recent one). The poorest awareness was for parental leave (another statutory right), especially at Castle Funds where it was not included in the staff handbook.

Employee awareness of flexible working practices

We also tested employee awareness of flexible working practices. The results are shown in Table 17. Of the policies that were formally available, awareness was high at North Bank, which had a flexible working policy. In fact, awareness was also high at Castle Funds; they were aware that flexible working policies were *not* available. Despite having the same policies, awareness was better at Edinburgh Life than at E-Bank. This could be because more people were making use of them (see section on 'Use of flexible working practices' below). However, it could also be the case that communication was more effective at Edinburgh Life, which relied on HR rather than line managers as the primary source of information.

The most interesting thing to note about these results is the fact that a significant minority of staff answered 'Yes, available at this workplace' to working arrangements which were not formally available. Dex and Smith (2002, forthcoming) also found this to be the case in their analysis of WERS 98. There are several possible explanations for this. First, the staff were possibly mistaken about policy

Table 16 Awareness of family leave policies – respondents saying 'Yes, available at this workplace'*

	Castle Funds	Edinburgh Life	E-Bank	North Bank
Time off for domestic emergencies (%)	69	60	63	74
Parental leave (%)	32	58	52	51
Paternity leave (%)	75	80	79	65
Compassionate leave (%)	85	88	88	77
N	119	181	160	73

Source: Staff surveys.

*All of these policies are formally available.

Table 17   Awareness of flexible working practices – respondents saying 'Yes, available in this workplace'

	Castle Funds	Edinburgh Life	E-Bank	North Bank
Flexitime (formal) (%)	5*	98	17*	22*
Flexibility of working hours (informal) (%)	40*	60*	46*	60*
Job sharing (%)	37*	77	38	78
Changing contracted hours (%)	47*	88*	72*	85
Career break (%)	9*	80	71	82
Term-time only contracts (%)	2*	7*	9*	15*
Home working (%)	29*	23*	8*	9*
Phased return from maternity leave (%)	34*	31*	34*	24*
N	119	181	160	73

Source: Staff surveys.

*Not formally available.

provision, showing ineffective communication of policies. Second, there may have been confusion over terminology. Respondents at E-Bank perhaps confused the shift-swapping system for flexitime. At North Bank, similar mistakes may have been made with their system of banking extra hours and taking them off in lieu. Finally, although the policies were not formally available, managers perhaps used their discretion to make them available to staff. Obviously, this was the case with informal flexibility of hours but it could also apply to job share, home working and phased return from maternity leave (although this could have been mistaken for return from maternity leave on part-time hours). In the case of changing contracted hours, although there was no formal policy in the staff handbook, at Edinburgh Life and E-Bank there were procedures in place to facilitate this process. No such procedures existed at Castle Funds and managers were generally unwilling to exercise their discretion in this way (see section on 'Changing contracted hours' later in this chapter).

Use of family leave policies

This section looks at the reported take-up by employee respondents of family leave policies in the last year. Findings for each leave arrangement are shown in Table 18.

Parental leave

The take-up of parental leave was very low. The restriction for children born on or after 15 December 1999 probably meant the few parents to whom it applied had not yet had a chance to take it. However, at Edinburgh Life and E-Bank, this restriction had been lifted and the age limit extended to eight years. Many managers, including HR, stated that they thought uptake was low because it was not

Table 18　Respondent use of family leave arrangements

	Castle Funds	Edinburgh Life	E-Bank	North Bank
Parental leave (%)	0.8	1.1	2.4	1.3
Time off for domestic emergencies (%)	12	11	11	12
Compassionate leave (%)	16	12	21	6
Paternity leave (%)	8	1.6	2	0
N	119	181	160	73

Source: Staff surveys.

paid. It was also the least familiar leave arrangement to employees across the four companies (see Table 16). However, a few respondents indicated they had used parental leave in the last year. There is a cautionary note attached to these findings in that respondents may have confused parental with maternity and paternity leave, despite the fact that they were clearly defined in the questionnaires. We found that, during interviews, line managers often confused these terms.

Time off for domestic emergencies (TODE)

In the case of time off for domestic emergencies, employee responses can be compared with evidence from line managers on how they operate formal policies (details in Table 10 in Chapter 5) within the constraints identified in Chapter 6.

This policy is examined in more depth as it provides a good illustration of how managers and staff utilise other leave and working time policies to find alternatives to the formal (unpaid or only partly paid) provision.

Reported usage among respondents was similar across the four companies, around 11–12 per cent of respondents, although managers demonstrated very different ways of operating the policy (details in Table 10 in Chapter 5). Line manager interviewees all stated that they would allow time off for any domestic emergency, although emergencies involving dependants tended to attract more sympathy. There was no statistically significant difference in the use of TODE by gender. However, parents were more likely to use this form of leave than non-parents.

At Castle Funds, managers used their discretion to extend the absence period and to make it paid. Employees here were the least likely to use sick leave to cover a non-work emergency (5 per cent) and none of these cases was connected to a care responsibility. They also reported the lowest proportion of employees having used holiday entitlement to cover a care responsibility (17 per cent). Of the 12 per cent of respondents who had taken emergency leave, all had been paid for the time taken off.

Employees at Castle seem to be able to get paid time off for domestic emergencies without too much trouble, although the longer working hours may explain this apparently generous approach (see section on 'Working hours culture' in Chapter 6):

People work hard here and will happily work an extra half-hour here or there so I generally think that Castle Funds win in the end.

(Castle Funds Director and HoD)

At Edinburgh Life, a range of working time practices rather than leave policies were used in order to deal with domestic emergencies:

They can take it out of their flexitime, holidays, work it up later, if they are part-time they might swap days. In extreme emergencies they can just have time off, it might be paid or we can just do unpaid leave but that isn't a formal policy ... Most people will actually offer to take holidays or to work it off.

(Edinburgh Life Customer Service Manager)

Five out of seven of the line manager interviewees stated that they would approach a request in a similar way and were not even aware of the formal entitlement. There was also the lowest level of awareness among employee respondents (60 per cent).

Unsurprisingly, Edinburgh Life had the highest instance (28 per cent) of respondents using their holiday leave in order to deal with domestic emergencies and the lowest use of emergency leave (11 per cent) with four-fifths of those instances being paid. Some managers noted that employees were used to managing their working time through the formal flexitime system and did not 'expect' an extra day off. Rather than request an extra day off, they would phone in and offer to take time out of flexi or holidays. Thirteen per cent of respondents stated that they had used paid sick leave to deal with a non-work emergency. The HR manager stated that the right to unpaid emergency leave should act only as a 'safety net' for those who do not have any holidays or flexitime left. However, this practice could

compound the stress experienced by those with care responsibilities:

All my holidays and flex leave are used up caring for young/disabled children, there's no space for 'R&R'.

(Edinburgh Life Customer Service Representative)

E-Bank has the same formal policy as Edinburgh Life with uptake (11 per cent) and rates of pay (four-fifths of cases were paid) revealed by the staff survey to be exactly the same. However, because of the lack of a flexitime system at E-Bank, other leave policies rather than working time practices were utilised as alternatives to the formal policy.

Some managers, including the HR Manager, were very clear that emergency leave should be unpaid despite the formal provision for managers to pay at their discretion. To get around this, employees sought to have the emergency classed under compassionate leave, which allowed for paid time off in the event of a serious illness of a dependant. Problems arose because managers did not interpret 'serious illness' consistently despite clarification attempts by HR and ELSA. One employee was told that she could not have paid time off when her daughter was undergoing major surgery because it was as a result of an accident and not a serious illness. However, many employees were successful in getting paid time off through this route. Over a fifth of respondents had taken compassionate leave in the last year, which was the highest usage of this arrangement in any of the companies. Fewer employees take time out of their paid annual leave to cope with a care responsibility, although the figure was still quite high with 24 per cent of the workforce doing so. E-Bank had the highest proportion of employees taking sick leave to deal with a non-work emergency at 17 per cent. The HR Manager recognised that people did this because emergency leave was not paid.

At North Bank, although 12 per cent of respondents had taken TODE, employees were also asked to make the time up later, take holiday or lieu days. Using holidays for care responsibilities was at a similar rate to E-Bank and Edinburgh Life at 26 per cent. The use of sick leave to deal with a non-work emergency was 14 per cent.

What really differentiated North Bank from the other case studies was an informal 'policy' to ask employees to share the sick dependant's care between them and their partner. However, there were some indications that employees did not consent to this:

> For a child's illness, I think you can reasonably expect the child-care arrangements to be split equally between two partners. If one partner takes the first day off and we pay it and the other takes a paid day off from his/her company and then if more time is required we would look at them taking holidays, lieu days or making time up. You have to look at the other partner, whether male or female, because you can't expect one company to carry all the weight.
>
> (North Bank Assistant Branch Manager, line manager interview)

> A policy of parents sharing time off if a child is ill has been introduced … As my husband is the main wage earner, I would be uncomfortable asking him to take time off to look after our children.
>
> (North Bank Employee, staff survey)

Evidence of the company interfering in the private division of care decisions was found in three of the case study branches. It was not formalised in the staff handbook but was partially supported by the requirement under special leave for employees to notify managers of alternative carers when requesting time off, although it was not specified what managers could do with this information.

Compassionate leave

As we have seen above, compassionate leave was commonly used at E-Bank (21 per cent), often as an alternative to TODE which was unpaid. According to the Human Resources Manager:

> There are two codes – emergency leave which is unpaid and compassionate leave which is paid. They [line managers] will put it through as compassionate leave if it's paid.
>
> (E-Bank HR Manager)

Compassionate leave at North Bank was less frequently used (4 per cent) possibly because there was provision for TODE to be at least partially paid.

There was no statistically significant difference in usage of compassionate leave by gender or by parental status.

Paternity leave

The reported and recorded incidences of paternity leave were not high in Edinburgh Life or E-Bank, and had not been used at all at North Bank where over four-fifths of staff were women. However, considering the relatively small number of employees at Castle Funds, quite a high proportion had taken paternity leave, possibly because 42 per cent of male respondents there had children, compared to only 15 per cent of female respondents.

Use of flexible working practices

Table 19 shows the use of flexible working practices as reported by survey respondents.

Formal flexitime

There was some confusion over the term 'flexitime' as Edinburgh Life was the only organisation to have a formal flexitime scheme, although 13 respondents from the other organisations thought that they had used it. The possible reasons for this confusion are outlined earlier in this chapter in the section on 'Employee awareness of flexible working practices'.

Informal flexibility of working hours

Despite the fact that managers at all the organisations, apart from Edinburgh Life, thought that a formal flexitime system was not workable because of the nature of the job (see section on 'Nature of the job' in Chapter 6), informal flexibility was reported to be used quite widely in all organisations. Managers were using their discretion to allow a certain amount of flexibility in the working day, although they were not keen, for operational reasons, to pass that control over to employees with a flexitime system. Informal flexibility was used slightly less at Castle Funds where it was mainly available to more senior staff (see section on 'The time factor' in Chapter 6). Where flexitime existed, there was some evidence to suggest that use of informal flexibility was less common.

There was no statistically significant use of flexibility of working hours based on gender or parental status.

Table 19   Respondents' use of flexible working arrangements in the last year

	Castle Funds	Edinburgh Life	E-Bank	North Bank
Flexitime (formal) (%)	2	90	3	8
Flexibility of working hours (informal) (%)	19	30	30	27
Job sharing (%)	2	2	1	3
Changing contracted hours: full time to part time (%)	2	7	4	4
Changing contracted hours: part time to full time (%)	0	1	1	8
Career break (%)	2	1	0	1
Term-time only contracts (%)	0	0	0	0
Home working (%)	2	3	0	0
Phased return from maternity leave (%)	0	0	1	0
N	119	181	160	73

Source: Staff surveys.

Changing contracted hours

The highest proportion of changes to contracted hours were at North Bank (12 per cent and mostly from part time to full time), where there was a 'flexible working policy' which pledged company support for employees changing their working patterns. Edinburgh Life had the next highest proportion of employees changing their hours (8 per cent). Managers at this organisation had a relaxed attitude towards employees changing their hours because of the high level of employee substitutability both in term of numbers and skills (see section on 'Substitutability' in Chapter 6). Slightly fewer employees (5 per cent) had changed their hours at E-Bank. At Castle Funds, two employees reported having changed their hours. Managers at this organisation were the least receptive towards flexible working (see section on 'Managers' attitudes to flexible working practices' in Chapter 6).

Women were much more likely to change hours from full time to part time than men. Parents were also much more likely to change hours from full time to part time. There were also more women than men changing hours from part time to full time, but this was not statistically significant because of the small numbers involved. The same number of parents and non-parents had changed from part time to full time.

Other flexible working arrangements

Phased return from maternity leave was not a formal policy in any of the organisations, although this was used once at E-Bank, presumably under managerial discretion.

The numbers of respondents who were *job sharing* was very limited in all companies (less than 3 per cent).

A small number of respondents indicated they had taken a *career break*, including two at Castle Funds.

Home working was uncommon in the case study organisations. No respondents at E-Bank or North Bank had worked from home, probably because of the customer-facing nature of the work. Only a small proportion at Castle Funds and Edinburgh Life had worked from home (2.5 per cent and 2.8 per cent respectively).

A note on respondent-reported versus company-recorded usage

We asked the HR Department in each of the organisations to provide their recorded take-up figures of FFPs. On the whole, where these were available, they broadly followed the patterns of those reported by survey respondents. However, there was some evidence that managers were not consistent in their recording of staff leave, in particular where they had used their discretion. The proportion of employee respondents who reported having used time off for domestic emergencies was much higher than on company records. Even at Edinburgh Life, where managers can 'code' a paid day off at manager's discretion on their staff attendance system, managers may be allowing staff time off without recording it. At E-Bank and North Bank, a system was used where managers had to 'code' the reasons for staff absences. At E-Bank, the HR Manager was aware that the system was not being properly used as one manager had given a woman paternity leave! Managers at Castle Funds did not have a system of recording and would only feedback to Personnel if the leave was for a longer time period. Given these practices and the evidence we found on lack of awareness and confusion over policies, HR at all four companies may not be getting reliable feedback on policy usage.

Employee access to family-friendly policies

The staff survey asked respondents if there were any family leave arrangements or flexible working practices they would have liked to have taken in the last year but did not, regardless of whether or not they were available. They were also asked if they had actually requested any of these and had been refused.

Access to family leave

Respondents were asked if there were any family leave arrangements (e.g. parental leave, TODE, paternity leave, compassionate leave) that they would have liked to have taken off in the last year but didn't for whatever reason. They were also asked if they had been refused any time off during this period. Table 20 shows the results.

The results show that there were very few respondents ($n = 40$) who felt that they did not have access to the family leave they would like. However, a higher proportion of respondents, particularly at Edinburgh Life, reported being refused time off.

Across the four companies, the most frequently mentioned family leave provision that respondents would have liked to have taken but didn't was time off for domestic

emergencies ($n = 27$). A small number also mentioned parental leave ($n = 7$) and compassionate leave ($n = 9$). No respondents mentioned paternity leave. The reasons why respondents had not taken family leave arrangements were varied, although those most frequently mentioned were 'not a formal entitlement' ($n = 11$), despite the fact that these leave policies are available at all four companies. There were no discernible differences between companies.

Employees were also asked if they had ever been refused time off. Of the 73 who had, the most frequently mentioned reason for wanting time off was for a holiday ($n = 47$), although 21 employees also mentioned that they wanted the time to spend with their family. At Castle Funds, the only time any respondents had been refused time off was for a holiday. At Edinburgh Life, a total of 33 respondents had been refused time off; while the majority said this had been for a holiday, nearly half (15) mentioned that they had wanted to spend time with their family. At E-Bank, 21 respondents had been refused time off and the vast majority of these had requested time off for a holiday. At North Bank, eight had requested time off, the reasons for which varied.

At Castle Funds, the main reason for being refused time off was split evenly between 'too

Table 20 Employees who would have liked to have taken family leave or time off in the last year				
	Castle Funds	Edinburgh Life	E-Bank	North Bank
Would have liked to have taken but didn't (%)	5	9	6	11
Refused time off (%)	9	19	13	11
N	119	181	160	73

much work to do' and 'no cover for my job' or 'maximum number of people off already'. At Edinburgh Life, E-Bank and North Bank, the predominant reason mentioned was 'no cover for my job' or 'maximum number of people off already'.

Edinburgh Life had the highest proportion of staff being refused time off despite having the highest level of staff substitutability, which managers used to their advantage when managing other working time practices (see section on 'Substitutability' in Chapter 6). However, if we look at the reasons for wanting time off at Edinburgh Life, nearly half of those being refused wanted to spend time with their families. This suggests that they were asking for leave during the school holidays when a lot of other staff were already off. Allowing staff their first choice of holiday leave had to be balanced with operational demands with many employees requesting to be off at the same time.

Access to flexible working

Survey respondents were asked if there were any flexible working arrangements (e.g. flexitime, flexibility of working hours, job sharing, changing contracted hours, career break, term-time only contracts, working at home or phased return from maternity leave)

that they would have liked to have taken in the last year but didn't. All respondents were also asked if they had been refused a change in their working pattern during this period. These questions deliberately did not differentiate between arrangements that were formally available and those that were not because: (1) respondents may not have been aware of what was formally available, and; (2) some arrangements may not have been formally available but may have been individually negotiated with line managers. Therefore, respondents were being asked about what arrangements they would have liked to have taken, or were refused, irrespective of whether these were actually formally available. The results, by company, are shown in Table 21.

Proportionally, more employees in all of the organisations felt they did not have access to the flexible working arrangements they would like. Significantly more felt the same way about family leave. However, very few of them who had actually requested leave had been refused.

A significantly higher proportion of employees at Castle Funds would have liked to have taken an arrangement, with the majority ($n = 14$) mentioning flexitime. Nine employees wanted to work at home. These results are not surprising given that they had no provisions for flexible working and a management

Table 21 Employees who would have like to have taken a flexible working arrangement

	Castle Funds	Edinburgh Life	E-Bank	North Bank
Would have liked to have taken but didn't (%)	27	11	14	17
Refused arrangement (%)	3	1	9	3
N	119	181	160	73

predominantly opposed to flexible working arrangements (see section on 'Managers' attitudes to flexible working' in Chapter 6).

At Edinburgh Life, where flexitime was in place, only 20 respondents mentioned that they would like to have taken some form of flexible working. There were various forms of working arrangements that respondents would have liked to have taken, although most popular were term-time contracts ($n = 7$).

Twenty-three E-Bank respondents indicated they would like more flexible working with the majority of these wanting flexitime ($n = 17$). Significantly more respondents had been refused a change to their working pattern. These respondents usually asked for a change to their shift patterns, or, for instance, not to work Saturdays. The main reason they had been given for not being able to do so was business needs.

At North Bank, 12 mentioned they would like to change their working arrangement, with the most often mentioned being flexitime ($n = 5$) or flexibility of working hours ($n = 5$).

The predominant reason that respondents across all organisations specified for not taking a particular working practice was because it was not a formal entitlement ($n = 64$).

Gender differences

We were interested to find out whether gender affected access to family leave and flexible working practices. The results are shown in Table 22.

A greater proportion of female employees in all four companies would have liked to have taken a family leave measure than males. However, when it came to having an actual request for time off refused, there were no differences between men and women, indicating that women were possibly less keen to ask for family leave than men.

There were no differences between males and females in the incidence of wanting to take a flexible working arrangement; however, men were more likely to report being refused access to this form of arrangement. This perhaps illustrates that it is perceived to be less acceptable for men to change their hours.

Parental status

A significantly higher proportion of parents than non-parents reported that they would have liked to have taken some form of family leave. Also, parents were slightly more likely to be refused this time off. Parents were also more likely to want to change their working

Table 22 Who is not able to take family leave and flexible working practices, by gender

	Male	Female
Family leave		
Would have liked to have taken but didn't (%)	4	10
Refused time off (%)	14	14
Flexible working practice		
Would have liked to have taken but didn't (%)	17	16
Refused arrangement (%)	6	3
N	192	339

practices than non-parents. They were also more likely to be refused a change in working practice (see Table 23).

Summarising the employee experience

• Employee representatives were perceived to be the least important source of information on FFPs. Perhaps the usefulness of these representatives was being limited by their lack of training, as previously noted.

• Awareness of the statutory rights for unpaid parental leave and time off for dependants was quite poor. Company initiatives on paid compassionate and paid paternity leave had much better levels of awareness.

• The lowest uptake of family leave was for parental leave. This was probably due to its very recent availability and lack of paid provision.

• Managerial discretion, working practices and organisational culture had a considerable impact on the way in which time off for domestic emergencies was operated.

• Managerial discretion had a major impact on access to flexible working practices with

many respondents reporting taking arrangements that were not formally available.

• Few respondents reported that they did not have access to the family leave they would have liked. Most of these wanted time off for domestic emergencies.

• Significantly more employees felt that they did not have access to a flexible working practice. Most of these respondents wanted flexitime.

• Gender was not an important variable in the uptake of *any* of the family-friendly policies except that women were more likely than men to change their contracted hours.

• Men were more likely to be refused access to a flexible working arrangement. Women were more likely to feel that they did not have access to the family leave they wanted.

• Parents were more likely than non-parents to take time off for a domestic emergency and to change the working hours. They were also more likely to feel that they did not have access to a flexible working arrangement and more likely to be refused.

Table 23   Who is not able to take family leave and flexible working practices, by parental status

	Parents	Non-parents
Family leave		
Would have liked to have taken but didn't (%)	13	5
Refused time off (%)	17	12
Flexible working practice		
Would have liked to have taken but didn't (%)	25	13
Refused arrangement (%)	8	2
N	159	372

9 | Company family-friendly performance

We have already seen that the individual employee experience is different in each organisation but how do companies perform *overall*? It was highlighted in Chapter 5 that managers perceived that family-friendly policies could help with recruitment and retention by providing flexibility and improving morale. Is this the case?

Outcomes

This section examines indicators of outcomes for the different approaches to family-friendly employment. The outcomes presented are based on the perceptions of survey respondents (including employees and managers) of the main advantages of FFPs, namely improved morale (as indicated by employee–management relations), retention and overall employee attitudes to company family-friendly provision.

Employee–management relations

Respondents were asked to describe relations between managers and employees at their workplace. On the whole, as Table 24 shows, responses were positive across all organisations.

Castle Funds respondents reported the highest levels of satisfaction with their relationship with their manager. This could be because it is a relatively small company with a high proportion of professionals. Relations were the poorest at E-Bank where managers had the least experience and the main operational activity was located in the call centre.

Managers in the organisations did not score quite so highly when it came to 'Dealing with work problems I may have', although over 58 per cent in each company rated managers as being good or very good in respect to this. There were no statistically significant differences between companies. Neither were there any differences between companies when it came to 'Treating employees fairly', with all of them scoring at least 61 per cent.

Retention

One frequently cited reason for the introduction of family-friendly and flexible working arrangements is to recruit and retain staff. While we were not able to examine the extent to which potential staff were attracted by a company's provisions, we were able to ask staff their *three* main reasons for staying with the company. Table 25 shows the proportion of respondents who mentioned the key factors among their top three reasons for staying.

The reason to stay in their company mentioned by the greatest percentage of

Table 24	Relations between managers and employees			
	Good or very good (%)	Neither good nor poor (%)	Poor or very poor (%)	N
Castle Funds	85	8	7	119
Edinburgh Life	76	20	3	177
E-Bank	69	18	13	159
North Bank	74	18	8	73
Mean	74	18	8	528

Table 25   Reasons given for employees staying with the company: main three reasons stated

	Castle Funds (%)	Edinburgh Life (%)	E-Bank (%)	North Bank (%)
Pay	52	71	57	53
Promotion prospects	26	24	34	16
Type of work	64	38	28	32
Company location	20	29	23	38
Company's reputation	21	33	47	21
The range of company benefits	25	21	31	22
Flexible working arrangements	3	30	6	8
To balance work and family life	7	12	8	40
No other suitable employment	7	19	19	26
Friendships established with workmates	19	14	26	7

respondents at Castle Funds was type of work (64 per cent), which perhaps contributed to the positive relationship with management. At Edinburgh Life, E-Bank and North Bank, the most cited reason for staying was pay.

Balancing work and life was cited by only a small minority of respondents with the exception of North Bank (40 per cent). The way in which employees here balanced their work and life was probably by working part time as North Bank had the highest use of part-time hours at 38 per cent.

Flexible working arrangements were cited by only a small proportion of staff, with the exception of Edinburgh Life (30 per cent). The most likely explanation for this is that many respondents at Edinburgh Life value the flexitime system that was available to them.

Apart from these two instances, staff valued other company benefits more highly than work–life balance and flexible working. However, the results for North Bank and Edinburgh Life show that, where companies provide the policies that employees want, those policies were valued.

Employee attitudes towards company FFPs

Respondents were asked to indicate how the company dealt with a number of work–life issues. The results are shown in Table 26.

Across the four organisations, respondents reacted reasonably positively to the statement 'Managers here are understanding about employees having to meet family responsibilities.' Compared to these results, respondents rated their *immediate* boss more favourably than managers in their company generally since at least 70 per cent said they agreed or strongly agreed that 'My immediate boss is sympathetic about personal matters.' These findings are reassuring given that the practice in all four organisations was to leave decisions to line managers, as they were able to take into account individual circumstances.

There were significant differences between

Table 26 How does the company handle work–life issues? Percentage agreeing or strongly agreeing

	Castle Funds	Edinburgh Life	E-Bank	North Bank
'Managers here are understanding about employees having to meet family responsibilities' (%)	65	59	67	63
'My immediate boss is sympathetic about personal matters' (%)	81	77	83	70
'This organisation is flexible when it comes to employees having to take time off at short notice for domestic or family reasons' (%)	81	67	67	51
'To get ahead here employees are expected to put their jobs before their families' (%)	31	46	30	45
'This is a "family-friendly" place to work' (%)	47	52	56	45
N	118	178	159	73

Source: Staff surveys.

organisations when it came to respondents ratings on 'This organisation is flexible about employees having to take time off at short notice for domestic or family reasons.' Castle Funds was rated to be the most flexible in allowing time off. This organisation did not have a formal TODE policy and relied on the discretion of managers who, in the main, allowed this time off to be paid. North Bank, which had the most formalised policy, was rated the least flexible. Managers complained that they were finding FFPs difficult to operate because of low staffing levels. The lack of flexibility could also be attributed in part to the 'policy' of requesting that employees' partners share the care burden and managers taking into account an employee's input of additional time when making a decision on a request for

TODE. Despite very different approaches to the same formal policy, Edinburgh Life and E-Bank scored exactly the same.

North Bank and Edinburgh Life had the highest proportions of staff agreeing that 'To get ahead employees were expected to put their jobs before their families.' These results are surprising given that these two companies had the most extensive use of flexible working, including in managerial posts. In fact, at North Bank, managerial job share was positively encouraged. Equally surprising is the fact that considerably fewer respondents at Castle Funds, the company with no provision for flexible working and the longest working hours, thought that to get ahead an employee had to put work first. However, the demographics of Castle Funds show that 60 per cent of respondents (all male) with dependent children considered their partner to be the primary carer. The figure at Edinburgh Life was 25 per cent indicating that employees at Castle Funds were less likely to be in a position where care responsibilities conflicted with work.

Overall, approximately half of all respondents felt that their organisation was a 'family-friendly place to work'. Male and female respondents in the four companies were evenly balanced in their responses to this question. Only in Edinburgh Life was there a different pattern of response between parents and non-parents, with 36 per cent of parents replying that their workplace was family-friendly, compared with 59 per cent of non-parents. There is no obvious explanation for this difference.

Summarising company family-friendly performance

- Overall, the relationship between managers and employees was perceived as being positive by over three-quarters of respondents.

- Forty per cent of respondents at North Bank reported that an important reason for staying with the company was to balance work and family life, most likely by working part time. Thirty per cent of Edinburgh Life respondents stated one of the reasons for staying with the company was the flexible working arrangements. Although there was no firm evidence that FFPs improved retention, it was clear from these results that, where companies did provide the policies employees wanted, these policies were valued.

- Respondents rated their immediate boss as being more sympathetic about personal matters than managers in the organisation generally.

- Castle Funds was rated the most flexible organisation in allowing employees time off at short notice for domestic or family reasons. It also had the least formal policy.

- A large minority of staff in each of the organisations agreed that to get ahead they would have to put their work before their family.

- Approximately half of all respondents thought that their organisation was a family-friendly place to work.

10 | Conclusions

SMEs

A number of specific conclusions emerge from the findings that contribute to a broader understanding of the development of family-friendly policies and the processes and practices that emerge from these policies. The specific conclusions can be summarised as follows:

- The review of broad policy-making dimensions of family-friendly working in 17 financial services companies supports the findings of other research that trade unions do make a difference. Nevertheless, the study reveals that voluntarily determined family-friendly policies have rather a long way to go before they make a significant impact in changing family-friendly employment conditions. Notwithstanding current policy concern with reconciling work and family life, our conclusions rather echo those of Lewis and Lewis five years ago in that 'these policies have not brought about fundamental changes in organizational behaviours or values' (Lewis and Lewis, 1996, p. 160).

- Where unions were recognised, there appeared to be a spread of initiatives and these initiatives were codified, for example, in staff handbooks. The quality of the initiatives, for example in terms of paid days off, seemed to be higher than in companies with staff association representation, a point not noted previously in the literature. Further, companies with trade unions accepted the obligation to discuss policies (or lack of them) formally with union representatives, offering further opportunities for unions to incorporate changes into terms and conditions of employment. Smaller companies that did not recognise trade unions or staff

associations but were faced with the necessity to recruit and retain specialised staff under competitive conditions have introduced a variety of policies, often informal, and largely operated under management discretion. These findings of informal and pragmatic developments are consistent with those found in Dex and Scheibl's (2001) examination of flexible and family-friendly working in SMEs. In at least some of the companies examined, there were dangers associated with such loose arrangements in that staff may not be treated equally or consistently. Further, 'concessions' may be easily withdrawn if business conditions or demands for labour change.

- Legislation has acted as a stimulus for many of the companies to review their family-friendly provisions. However, where companies had previously been offering conditions above the new legislative provisions, some were reluctant to progress beyond these new statutory levels, though other companies will have to catch up.

- Only two of the 17 companies stated that they were moving in a family-friendly direction primarily in order to help their staff achieve balance between their working and domestic lives. All the companies were motivated largely by business competitive concerns and the need to meet at least minimal statutory requirements. Some respondents pointed out they were keen to avoid the (business damaging) bad publicity that might result from an industrial tribunal appearance.

- For business reasons also, the evidence indicated a far more extensive spread of flexible working practices compared to family-friendly policies. The influence of business needs also spread into the operation of FFPs where considerable discretion was given to line managers over a range of initiatives at the individual employee level.

- From these management accounts, there was little evidence offered of active or concerted union campaigns in the direction of FFPs in the companies. Union full-time officers, however, were adamant that pursuit of FFPs was a priority objective generally as well as with specific employers included in the sample of companies. Nevertheless, unions expressed reservations not only about managerial resistance but also about the perceived apathy of members. From the company survey, there also appeared to be evidence of indifference or inhibitions among staff, demonstrated, for example, by the lack of response to the pilot nursery scheme in one of the banks.

- Few of the companies voluntarily drew attention to family-friendly issues. For example, many of the companies organised regular staff attitude surveys, yet very few of these made any explicit reference in their questionnaires to work–life balance or to links between domestic and work lives.

- It was clear from management accounts at the 17 companies that, whilst a range of company policies was in place, there was ample scope to interpret these policies in the workplace. It is also apparent that this scope was a major factor when it came to translating policies into actual practices. The intention of the case study phase was to illuminate and explain both the processes and outcomes of these interpretations. The

four case studies confirmed the broad areas of practice open to line manager discretion even in a company such as North Bank where union involvement in corporate policy was acknowledged to be well established and policies were more precisely defined.

- The company case studies revealed that voluntary initiatives taken by companies were not profound and that relatively few employees have taken advantage of the limited entitlements on offer.

- The resources from which line managers drew their authority in this area were somewhat questionable. It appeared that, in some of the companies at least, line managers and team leaders with responsibilities in work allocation were inexperienced and lacked awareness in dealing with staff with family responsibilities. Many had received little or no recent training in issues of work–life balance, whether from a company or statutory perspective. Many managers were clearly ignorant or confused about recent statutory developments. Perhaps in consequence of lack of training or poor communication, ignorance of these issues was widespread among managers. Managerial awareness was most apparent where policies pre-dated the Employment Relations Act 1999 and had clear and formal entitlements such as paternity and compassionate leave.

- Managers were also faced with potential tensions when exercising the considerable discretion open to them: they needed to tailor individual subordinate working time to operational needs. At the same time, consistency of treatment was a factor facing both individual managers in dealing with their staff and between managers with different groups of subordinate employees.

- Line managers tended to consult with their human resource colleagues only over non-routine family-related matters. Human resource specialists gave the impression that they would like managers to embrace and practise greater consistency in their treatment of staff. More broadly, HR managers would have liked companies to take strategic family-friendly agendas forward more forcefully; but there was little evidence that these largely advisory services had sufficient organisational authority to achieve either of these ambitions.

- A combination of factors fed into the managerial discretionary equation. Among these were: managerial attitudes, often linked to the nature of the jobs within their domain and in particular the degree of staff substitutability; temporal demands of the post set against availability of flexible working options; and perceived contributions of the job-holder to organisational needs, specifically in terms of time inputs. Some managers, at least, were suspicious of employee motives in requesting time off. A long hours culture, clearly inimical to family-friendly working, underpinned management (and to some extent employees') perceptions of appropriate work–life balances. In at least two companies, however, managers linked access to paid family leave to their perceptions of individual employees' levels of commitment to work unpaid beyond their contractual hours.

- Though trade unions can influence corporate level policy in terms of spread and codification of provisions, there was little evidence that representative arrangements or workplace union representatives themselves offered anything more than token contributions to the exercise of management discretion.

- In terms of experienced outcomes from the arrangements, there was little radical to observe. Only a tiny proportion of the 533 survey respondents in the four case studies reported job sharing, career breaks or working at or from home, with the latter treated more as a 'perk' rather than a contribution to family-friendly work. Comparatively few respondents have used any of the family leave arrangements on offer (especially parental leave) and a small but noticeable number would have liked to have taken leave that was not on offer but did not request it, or had their requests turned down.

- Gender was not an important variable in the uptake of family-friendly policies, though women were more likely than men to change their contracted working hours. They were also more likely than men to feel that they did not have access to the family leave they wanted.

- Taking time off for domestic emergencies (and who paid for it) was very much dependent on management discretion, working arrangements and organisational culture. Use of flexible working arrangements was more common and, as has been noted elsewhere, flexible working does not necessarily correspond with family friendliness (Purcell et al., 1999). However, employees generally expressed satisfaction at the apparent empathy of managers with their needs, though large minorities of respondents in all the companies felt that, to progress, employees were expected to put jobs before families.

- The overall impression was that, whilst forms of flexible working were well established and were managed reasonably sympathetically by managers, there had not been large advances in any of the companies in terms of restructuring the employment relationship in family-friendly directions. Much of the key operational decision-making was in the hands of line managers who acted pragmatically in the service of their organisations. Neither representative participation nor direct individual participation by employees appeared to have influenced these processes in any meaningful ways.

Implications for employers, trade unions and policy-makers

The study demonstrates the elusiveness of meaning attributable to being a 'family-friendly employer'. Unlike many organisations that label themselves as 'equal opportunity' employers, no companies in our studies openly or publicly proclaimed themselves as family friendly. Neither (unlike some Opportunity 2000 or Opportunity Now companies) did they set any form of targets towards accomplishing family friendliness or towards achieving desirable balances between work and family. Managers within the same companies would often offer very different interpretations as to the meanings of family friendliness within their companies, though a common tendency to identify family friendliness with flexible working was evident. Interestingly, the same confusion and definitional ambiguity was found among the small sample of trade union officers interviewed. This uncertainty does not help trade unions in their efforts to establish policies individually with employers or collectively in helping to determine the directions and contours of policy-making. One problem for bodies intent on raising the profile of family-friendly work is that it is not a substantive issue like pay, but a qualitative one whose boundaries are fluid and open to diverse interpretations.

Partly as a consequence of the above, a second general conclusion is that a main instrument of government policy, that of encouraging voluntary agreement between individual employees or groups of employees with their employer, is operating patchily and is largely dictated by company business demands mitigated by their requirements for labour. The union officers interviewed were sceptical about the motives of some employers, who try 'to get away with as little as possible' or do not consider family friendliness to be a priority.

The findings suggest that, if it is left to the employees and their representatives to agree enhancements to provisions, progress will not be profound. In any case, few employees will be able to exploit enhancements. Unpaid leave is unlikely to act as a catalyst in easing current workplace tensions with regard to family life. Employers do respond, however reluctantly, to statutory requirements and perhaps the unions, in common with the TUC, are being realistic in targeting the Government to give more teeth to its family-friendly policies through statutory reform. The extent to which the Government feels able to respond to this campaign is another question.

Note

Chapter 2

1 Military leave is offered to staff who undertake voluntary duties with one of the British armed forces.

References

Baldry, C., Bunzel, D., Hyman, J. and Marks, A. (2000) 'Get a life: "living the brand at work and home"', Employment Research Unit, Annual Conference, Cardiff

Bargaining Report (2000) No. 206

Bargaining Report (2001) No. 215

Bean, R. (1994) *Comparative Industrial Relations*. London: Routledge

Confederation of British Industry (1990) 'A nation of shareholders', *CBI News*, November, pp. 8–10

Crow, G. and Hardey, M. (1999) 'Diversity and ambiguity among lone-parent households in modern Britain', in G. Allan (ed.) *The Sociology of the Family*. Oxford: Blackwell

Cully, M., Woodland, S., O'Reilly, A. and Dix, G. (1999) *Britain at Work*. London: Routledge

Dex, S. and Scheibl, F. (1999) 'Business performance and family-friendly policies', *Journal of General Management*, Vol. 24, No. 4, pp. 22–37

Dex, S. and Scheibl, F. (2001) 'Flexible and family-friendly working arrangements in UK-based SMEs: business cases', *British Journal of Industrial Relations*, Vol. 39, No. 3, pp. 411–31

Dex, S. and Smith, C. (2002, forthcoming) *The Nature and Patterns of Family-friendly Policies in Britain*. York: YPS for the Joseph Rowntree Foundation

DTI (1997) *Partnerships with People*. London: DTI

DTI (2000) *Competitiveness and Choice: Research and Analysis*. London: DTI

Equal Opportunities Review (2000) August

Ermisch, J. and Francesconi, M. (2001) *The Effects of Parents' Employment on Children's Lives*. London: Family Policy Studies Centre

Forth, J., Lissenburgh, S., Callender, C. and Millward, N. (1997) *Family-friendly Working Arrangements in Britain*. Research Paper No. 16. London: Department for Education and Employment

Franks, S. (1999) *Having None of it: Women, Men and the Future of Work*. London: Granta

Harkness, S. (1999) 'Working 9 to 5?', in P. Gregg and J. Wadsworth (eds) *The State of Working Britain*. Manchester: Manchester University Press

Hogarth, T., Hasluck, C. and Pierre, G. (2000) *Work–Life Balance 2000: Baseline Study of Work–Life Balance Practices in Great Britain*. London: DfEE

Hyman, J., Baldry, C. and Bunzel, D. (2001) 'Balancing work and life: not just a matter of time flexibility', *Work, Employment and Society*, Conference, University of Nottingham, September

IRS Employment Trends (2000) Special Issue: 'Family-friendly employment, No. 697, February

Labour Research (2000) 'Who'll be at work in 2010?', Vol. 89, No. 1, pp. 17–18

Labour Research (2001) 'What working parents really need', Vol. 90, No. 3, pp. 10–13

Labour Research Department (2000) *Parental and Dependency Leave*. London: Labour Research Department

Lewis, S. and Lewis, J. (1996) 'Rethinking employment: a partnership approach', in S. Lewis and J. Lewis (eds) *The Work–Family Challenge*. London: Sage

Management Today (2000) 'Age of the Flex Exec', August, pp. 46–52

Purcell, K., Hogarth, T. and Simm, C. (1999) *Whose Flexibility?: The Costs and Benefits of 'Non-standard' Working Arrangements and Contractual Relations*. York: YPS for the Joseph Rowntree Foundation

Scottish Abstract of Statistics (1998) No. 26

Simpson R. (2000) 'Presenteeism and the impact of long hours on managers', in D. Winstanley and J. Woodall *Ethical Issues in Contemporary Human Resource Management*. Basingstoke: Macmillan

Sisson, K. and Storey, J. (2000) *The Realities of Human Resource Management*. Buckingham: Open University Press

Appendix 1: Telephone survey of finance sector unions – main issues covered

1   Details of union coverage and membership trends and profiles

2   Respondent designation and responsibilities

3   Union definition of FFPs and FWPs

4   Union objectives for FFPs

5   Training provided for officials and lay representatives

6   Coverage of FFPs at annual conferences

7   Approaches adopted with employers over FFPs

8   Relations between union and employers including constraints concerning FFPs

9   Interventions with employers on behalf of members, including tribunals

10 Input into policy-making, e.g. through submissions to Green Papers

11 Main union priorities with regard to the financial services sector

12 Financial services sector provision of FFPs and role of union

13 Family-friendly campaigns or promotions

14 Impact on members of family-friendly issues

Appendix 2: Approaches to FFP provision

Castle Funds

Family-friendly provision
Some paid leave beyond the statutory minimum but no provision for flexible working practices. Low levels of codification with most policies relying on managerial discretion. Some policies developed in response to requests from individuals.

Workplace characteristics
Longer working hours and little flexibility with 94 per cent of staff on full-time hours. Small workforce with a high proportion of professionals and therefore low employee substitutability. No objective evaluation had been carried out of which tasks were time critical, although many were not.

Managerial influence
High levels of managerial discretion with no one else involved in the decision-making process, although managers were wary of 'setting a precedent'. The prevalent view of flexible working was negative, i.e. that managerial posts were not suitable for part-time/job share, part-timers were difficult to manage and those who worked reduced hours were less committed to the organisation.

Involvement
Employee representatives had no influence in the introduction or operation of FFPs.

Uptake issues
Most time off for domestic emergencies (TODE) was paid and there were the lowest levels making use of sick and holiday leave to deal with domestic emergencies. The lowest use of FWPs was complemented by the highest levels of employees wanting to take FWPs (flexitime).

Edinburgh Life

Family-friendly provision
Some provision beyond statutory minimum including extended parental leave rights and other paid leave. Policies formalised but managerial discretion 'built in' to some. A range of flexible working practices was available including flexitime.

Workplace characteristics
High substitutability in terms of employee skills and numbers and non-time-critical tasks, which is why flexitime was workable.

Managerial influence
Managers were very comfortable about using their discretion and tailoring responses to each request. Open to flexible working and employees changing their working hours.

Involvement
The staff association, ELSA, had some role in extending leave rights such as parental and paternity but had no significant role in the operation of policies. Out of the four companies, employee

representatives had the highest proportion of staff rating them as the most important source of information on FFPs.

Uptake issues

Lowest levels of awareness for the TODE policy; other working time practices such as flexitime were employed instead. Highest usage of paid holidays to cover a care responsibility. Highest use of FWPs, especially flexitime, and the best access to and lowest levels of refusal of FWPs.

E-Bank

Family-friendly provision

The same provision as Edinburgh Life, although no flexitime available.

Workplace characteristics

Employees highly substitutable but the main activities were customer facing so tasks were time critical and working patterns were fixed. No flexitime but some informal flexibility and a shift-swap system. High proportion of full-time staff but the shortest overtime hours.

Managerial influence

Out of all four companies, managers were the least willing to use their discretion. Less experienced managers frequently consulted HR and were concerned with adherence to formal provision. Some negative attitudes to flexible working but culture changing. Relaxed about planning for family leave because of substitutability of staff.

Involvement

As Edinburgh Life, although employee representatives were used less as an information source.

Uptake issues

Highest rates of using other paid leave, compassionate and sick leave, to cover TODE. Employees who felt that they did not have access to an FWP wanted flexitime.

North Bank

Family-friendly provision

Higher levels of formalisation and guidance on using policies. Flexible working policy and some extra statutory paid leave.

Workplace characteristics

Low staffing levels in the branch network made FFPs sometimes difficult to operate. Customer-facing staff were on fixed working patterns. Second longest working hours as contracted hours do not cover full working day. High proportion of part-timers.

Managerial influence

Managers happy to use discretion and did not involve anyone else in the decision. Perceived employee input a criteria for access to paid leave.

Involvement

Union influence at policy level but very little involvement at operational level.

Uptake issues

Evidence of some managers asking employees who request TODE if their partners could share some of this. Highest proportion of staff wanting family leave but not taking it. Staff who wanted an FWP wanted flexitime or informal flexibility of hours.